TONY K. BURRIS
The Hero, The Person, The Letters

Compiled and Edited by
Larry W. Wilson, Editor
Lee Anne Hite, Co-editor
Teresa Ann Wilson, Co-editor

Tony K. Burris

The Hero, The Person,
The Letters

Compiled and Edited by

Larry W. Wilson,
Lee Anne Hite, Teresa Ann Wilson

PARKE
PRESS

DEDICATION

This book is dedicated to Loretta Wilson, sister of Tony,
mother of Teresa and Larry,
and grandmother of Lee Anne Hite.
The Burris family knew her affectionately as Sister Bea.

Book Design: Marshall Rouse McClure

Published by

PARKE PRESS

Norfolk, Virginia

ISBN 978-0-9883969-8-2

Library of Congress Control Number is available upon request

Printed in the United States of America

CONTENTS

Editor's Note

When I was three years old, my uncles Burnett and Tony rode horses to Blanchard and led me, Larry Wilson, around on a horse called Cherry. At the farm a few months later, they put me on that same mare and turned us loose. My Grandmother Burris came out of the house immediately to shut us down, loudly saying that horse was "way too dangerous." Unfortunately, I now have more memories of that horse[1] than of Tony. He joined the Army before I was eight years old and was home for only a few days after enlisting.

I have come to know Tony through family stories and posthumous honors, but primarily by reading his letters, transcribed here as written without correcting for spelling, punctuation, or grammar. The honors began with the Silver Star and the Medal of Honor. They have continued into the new millennium as Blanchard, the Choctaw Nation, the State of Oklahoma, veteran and military organizations, the U.S. government, the Korean government, and others continue to honor Tony. The purpose of this book is to share the letters and his story as widely as possible.

I would like to thank the Burris family and Pam Witt for making this book possible, by entrusting me with the letters, and supporting this project. I would also like to express my appreciation to Twila J. Wilson, my wife, who put up with me while providing invaluable real-time editing, feedback, and comments for this project.

Larry Wilson
Norfolk, Virginia

---

1 My memories of Cherry include being dumped on my head when she bolted to scrape me off on a fence post, and her biting or kicking me every time she had the opportunity. I now know, from Burnett, that she had once scratched Tony up by bolting through a thicket of bushes and blackjack trees in earlier times.

PREFACE

Tony K. Burris was born May 30, 1929 in Blanchard, Oklahoma. He enlisted at the start of the Korean War, and after four months of training was assigned to third platoon, Love Company, 3rd Battalion, 38th Infantry Regiment, 2nd Infantry Division of the 8th U.S. Army in late January 1951. Sergeant First Class Tony K. Burris died on Heartbreak Ridge near Mung Dung Ni, Korea on October 9, 1951. His military honors include a Purple Heart with two Oak Leaf Clusters, a Silver Star, and the Medal of Honor.

Tony sent over seventy letters to the Burris, Wilson, and Witt families during his fourteen months of service. These letters tell his story from basic training to Heartbreak Ridge. They provide insight into the life of a truly decent, Tabasco-loving, homesick young Choctaw doing his duty while trying to survive and maintain contact with his family and friends.

Young Tony

Tony was born just in time for the Great Depression and the Oklahoma Dust Bowl. The family lived on farms they did not own and worked as sharecroppers to survive. They were often hungry, particularly when drought or dust destroyed crops. In 1939, the family moved to a larger farm belonging to Tony's Aunt Jenny Curry Apple and her husband Harry, but still had trouble making ends meet. Their modest three-bedroom house did not have a phone or electricity until the early '40s. The family had an outhouse and carried water from an outdoor pump. With help from the older children, the Burris family planted large gardens and raised chickens, cows, and pigs. Tony also contributed by trapping rabbits and catching fish.

Pre-War Tony

Little brother Burnett described many adventures with his older brother Tony including "noodling,"[1] a high school prank, and a challenge:

While noodling, Tony came up holding a snake. Burnett laughed at him and asked, "What are you going to do with that?" Tony replied, "I am going to throw this &#@* thing as far as I can."

Tony, Burnett and seven others put Mr. McBride's cow in a classroom. This resulted in a trip to the police station for proper threats and intimidation.

Several years later, Burnett observed a man challenge Tony and a friend as they were leaving the Blanchard pool hall, saying "I've got five dollars that says I can whip both of you." Tony approached the man to say quietly, "I believe I'll have some of that five." The man walked away.[2]

---

1 They noodled by going underwater to grab catfish: once Tony nearly drowned, and another time friend Dickie Clanton lost a finger.

2 In the Choctaw Legacy film, *Tony K. Burris*, Billy Wilson, a childhood friend of Tony's says, "Tony was easygoing and pleasant, but if you wanted to get a little tough with him, he was ready."

Pruitt Lewis (pictured here), now a retired Blanchard School Superintendent, says, "I have never heard anyone say a bad thing about Tony Burris." He also describes in detail Tony's performance in the 1946 Junior Class Play:

Tony played a gruesome deranged killer who escaped from a mental institution to commit murder and mayhem. During the matinee performance for the K-12 student body, the younger students sat up front, close to the stage in a darkened auditorium. In the final scene, a detective, played by Red Mitchell, was to shoot Tony's character who would fall and die as the curtain dropped. Instead of falling, Tony leaped aggressively into the audience, creating chaos and hysteria, particularly amongst the younger students. Pruitt, in the eighth grade and sitting several rows back recalls, "As Tony ran up the aisle past me, he was grinning from ear to ear," and nearby School Superintendent Mac Starry murmured, "Tony, Tony, Tony." Pruitt concludes by saying, "I never will forget that as long as I live."

The Burris Family

Tony Kenneth Burris was the third of ten children born to Samuel **Sidney** and **Mable** Agnes Curry Burris. He grew up with older sisters **Loretta** Florence (1925) and **Wanda** Lou (1927), younger brother Sidney **Burnett** (1932), and sisters Joyce **Joan** (1935) and **Karen** Jane (1938). Eventually twin brothers Terry Doyce **"T.D."** and **Perry** Royce (January, 1945) and twin sisters Cathryn **Jen**nifer and Diana **Judy** (December, 1945) joined the family. Tony also considered Loretta's husband **Doyce** Wayne Wilson (1924), their son **Larry** Wayne (1942), Wanda's husband **Virgil** O. Witt (1925), and their daughter **Pam**ela Janet (1946) to be part of his family.

The Family. Back row (L-R) – Sid, Tony, Burnett with niece Pam on his shoulders, Mable. Middle Row – Karen, Wanda, Loretta, Joan. Front Row – Ralph Gamble (nephew of Sid), Perry, Judy, Jen, TD, Larry, and Pooch – December 1950.

Blanchard, Oklahoma

Tony grew up on a farm near Blanchard, a small farming community twenty-five miles southwest of Oklahoma City. Downtown was one block of Main Street. The west side contained a grocery store, pool hall, drugstore, five and dime, two department stores, and a bank. The east side included a Ford dealership, a movie theater, and a feed and seed store. Nearby were City Hall, the jail, the bus station, a lumberyard, a barbershop, filling stations, beer joints, and many churches.

Blanchard had a single school for all grades with about 20 students per grade. On Saturday families came to town for the children's matinee movie, followed by a drawing in which a lucky ticketholder might win a new pair of overalls or a frying pan.

Downtown Blanchard Parade – circa 1948

THE LETTERS

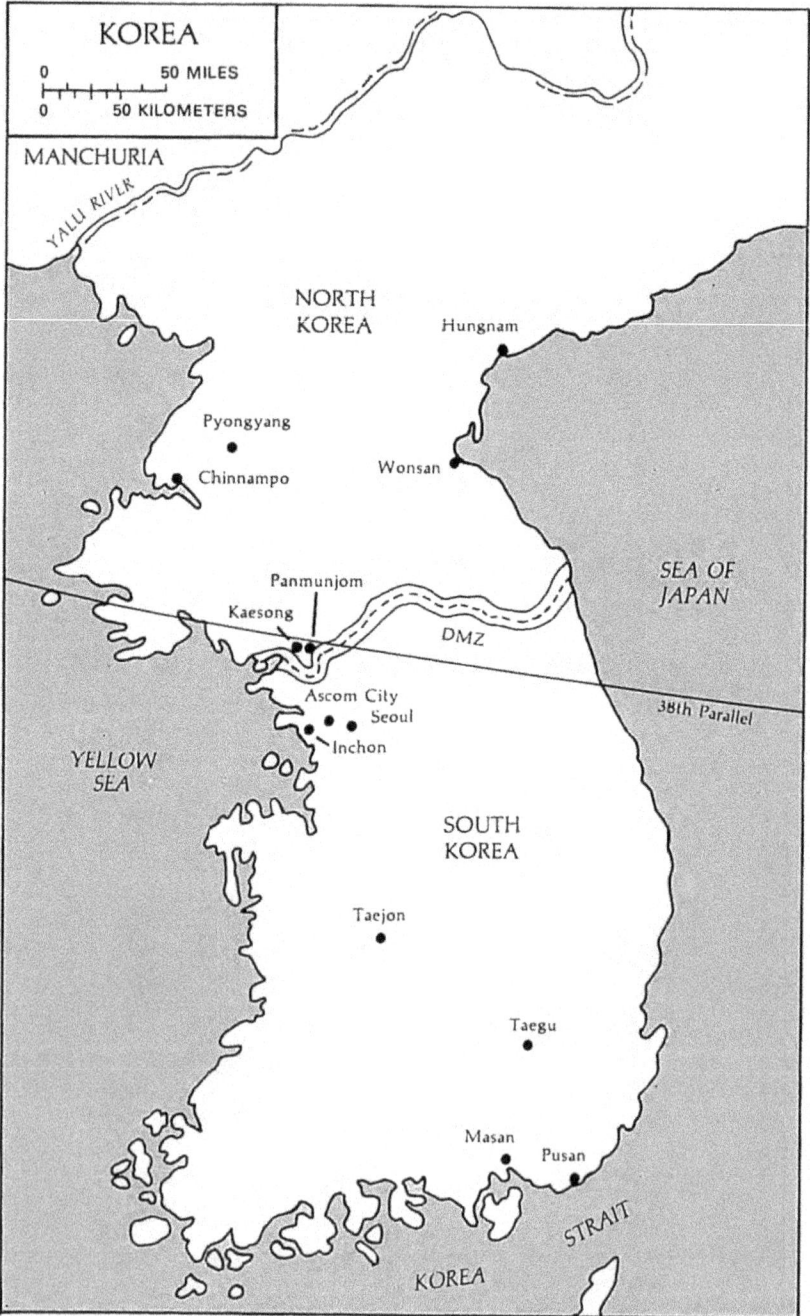

KOREA

0 _____ 50 MILES

0 _____ 50 KILOMETERS

MANCHURIA

YALU RIVLR

NORTH KOREA

Hungnam

Pyongyang

Chinnampo

Wonsan

Panmunjom

Kaesong

DMZ

SEA OF JAPAN

38th Parallel

Ascom City

Seoul

Inchon

YELLOW SEA

SOUTH KOREA

Taejon

Taegu

Masan

Pusan

STRAIT

KOREA

....

KOREAN WAR BEGINS SUDDENLY

....

NKPA invades ROK; Tony enlists

June 24: *Secretary of State Dean Acheson phones President Truman to inform the president that North Korea has invaded South Korea; four days later the North Korean People's Army (NKPA) captures Seoul, the capital of South Korea (ROK).*

June 30: *President Truman authorizes the use of ground forces in Korea.*

July 29: *General Walton Walker orders U.N. troops along the Pusan Perimeter "to stand or die" in a desperate effort to keep the NKPA from pushing them into the sea.*

Tony Burris and his friend Linard White enlist. On July 30, they are in basic training at Fort Riley, Kansas. Tony is hungry and wants to send money home.

....

July 30-50

Dear Mom, Dad, & kids,
I guess you'll had given me

Fort Riley, Kansas
July 30, 1950

Dear Mom, Dad, & kids,

I guess you'll had given me up writing. I haven't been able to get any stamps. How is all the family fine I hope. Sure wish I could eat one of those chicken dinners. I guess the army is alright but I don't seem to be able to get enough to eat. Who-ever said the army feeds plenty was nuts. I think it is because there are so many new recruits coming in and they aren't prepared for them. Most of the guys in my barracks are just seventeen and eighteen years old. They sort of look up to me. Is dad & Burnett still working. I hope so. They wouldn't let me sign up for dependents. Well its about time to eat so I'll have to close for now.

Write soon

Tony

••

3 Aug. 1950

Hi Folks [Wilson],

How is everyone doing? I've been sleeping since Sat. at noon the biggest part of the time. We got off duty for two and a half days but I understand we will probably make up for it the rest of this week by doing night work. We have about three more days bivouac and will have sham battles day and night they say. Well I did have to sleep with a colored boy last week but by the time we got off to go to bed it didn't bother me at all. One thing about it they have to stay as clean as anyone else in here. The darned chiggers nearly carried me off all week. They sure are thick here. I am sending you twenty dollars that I owe you for I may spend it or lose it if I try to keep it. But if I do get to come home soon on a leave I may need to borrow it right back if I don't I won't. I guess the kids are going to school by now aren't they? How is the Lumber yard business?[1] Still selling lots of lumber? Has Doyce[2] finished his houses? It seems like I can't think of anything to write except to ask questions so I'll close & let you do the writing.

Answer soon

Tony

....

Aug 9, 1950

Dear Mom, Dad, & Kids,

How is everyone doing? Me I'm doing ok. Linard White is in the barracks next door but I don't see a lot of him. We aren't allowed in each other's barracks. Our fourteen weeks basic here has been shortened to six so you can imagine how busy we are. After these six weeks we will be shipped elsewhere for some advanced combat training. I think possibly I'll be able to get a short leave after these six weeks are up which falls on the 11th of Sept. But don't plan

---

1 Tony had worked as a truck driver for Carey Lumber Yard where Loretta was employed as the bookkeeper.

2 Doyce built and sold houses on speculation. The Wilsons often lived in his new house until it sold.

on it too strongly as no one knows for sure yet. We have to put in a lot of hours to make up for those weeks we are missing but as you know I'm not used to getting much sleep anyhow. You should see some of these kids getting sick & falling out on our marches. I can understand why Burnett didn't like boot camp now but I've done just as hard or harder work just before coming in and am used to it. Of course these exercises they give us are using muscles that I am not used to using but the more I use them now the better condition I will be in for things that may happen in the future. It seems like everyone here is hurrying to get their letters written before time for the lights to go out. When they go out I'll go downstairs & take a cold shower, we don't have any hot water then go to bed. We will be restricted to the base for the six weeks we are here so I guess it wouldn't do much good for you all to come up. Anyhow if I'm lucky I'll be home shortly after the 11th. Well its about that time so I guess I'll sign off.

> **"I can understand why Burnett didn't like boot camp..."**

Write soon

Tony

•••

Aug. 13, 1950

Dear Bee, Doyce & Larry,

I suppose you had given up hearing from me but the way they are rushing us through basic I don't have much time to write. How is everyone getting along these days. Me I'm all right besides being a little sore in spots. We've been getting up at 4 o'clock & going to bed at nine so you can see we're kept pretty busy. There is a rumor going around camp that we may be shipped to another training center before the month is up so I don't know what to expect. Well it's very hot here now but at night it gets cool. Linard White is in the hospital. I think they are going to operate on him for the piles so I guess we will be separated. I'm restricted to company quarters so I can't even go see how he is doing. Well I think I'll close for now as it is very hot. Tell all the boys at the yard hello for me.

Write soon

Tony

Aug. 17, 1950

Dear Mom, Dad, & Kids,

How is everybody? Me I'm a shade tired. I can't seem to find much time to write so don't think much about it if this is a shade short. Linard is back out of the hospital now so we may get to stay together a while longer. I heard from "Bee" today. Well I wish I could be home for a few days but I wouldn't want to go back to work. I guess I'm lazy. Anyhow I've got 3 years to try to get it out of my system. I got tired rather tired of wanting to quit a job after a few months. So I got one I can't quit for a while possibly it will teach me something but I doubt. Has Dad found a job yet. I hope so. Is Burnett still working. Tell him he better work all he can. If I ever get a leave I might want to get drunk on him. Well I have to end this it's bedtime.

Write soon

Tony

Aug. 19, 1950

Dear "Bee", Doyce, & Larry,

How is everyone doing these days? Is the weather still warm? We've got a little cold streak here today. Someone just said it was supposed to freeze tonight. I will sure enough have a cold now. One day it will be so hot you sweat in the shade & the next you need your long handles. I saw Ramon Brooks the other day at the PX. He was going to Junction City when he left but I won't be able to for a few more weeks yet. Linard got out of the hospital and is back in the same company with me so maybe we will get to stay together. Unless the orders are changed we will ship out the 11th of Sept. But I don't much think I'll be able to get a leave then. A company left today for Fort Sill. It would be nice if I was sent there. Tell Joan I appreciated her letter but can't find any more news to write besides what I've written you and mom so she can read them. I've run out of news so I guess I'll close.

Write soon,

Tony

Sid, Tony, and Mable Burris (September 1950)

Tony and Burnett with Linard White

Burnett and Tony with Doyce Wilson

ELECTRONICS SCHOOL

U.N. forces take the offensive; Tony studies

September 15: *After being nearly pushed off the southern tip of Korea, the U.N. forces make an amphibious landing in Inchon. By September 28, the U.N. forces are in control of Seoul.*

At Ft. Belvoir, Tony tries to avoid work. He excels in early classes, but turns down an instructor position rather than delay a potential leave. He wins big in a dice game only to lose even more to a thief.

Inchon landing. Boats are stuck in the sand at low tide.

Hi Folks [Burris],

I suppose you will be surprised to hear from me after waiting so long but I'm getting too lazy to write. I thought maybe the army would get me out of this laziness but I'm getting worse every day. We arrived here Sunday & I've been dodging officers ever since to keep out of work. They catch me if I hang around the barracks so I have to hide elsewhere. So far I haven't had to do anything but I'm never up here in the barracks so I can write. My school starts a week from Monday & they try to make us cut grass & stuff like that while we aren't going to school. My buddy is stationed right across the street from me but I guess we will be split up when I start to school. Tell Bee & Wanda I will drop them a line when I get more energetic. I've just found out that I have to go on K.P. tomorrow and the K.P.s really have to work here. I guess it will be a rough old day. Has anyone heard from Linard? I'm afraid he is apt to be sent overseas before long, this camp he was sent to is supposed to be a shipping center for Europe. I was talking to a sargeant down here at this electric school yesterday. He said nearly everyone that had taken this course here was sent to Europe. I certainly hope I get sent there. This would be an awful long three years if I had to stay in the states. Well it's about chow time so I guess I'll close. I still don't miss my chow.

Tony

"The K.P.s really have to work here..."

Hi folks [Burris],

How is everyone doing? Me I'm all right. I start to school Monday. Is dad & Burnett working yet? I hope so because I need some money. I got my check the other day and got in a dice game that night. When I got up I had $260 in my billfold. I guess one of the guys that went broke watched me hide it. Anyhow the next morning my pillowcase had a hole cut in it and I didn't have a billfold. So if they have a couple of dollars that I can buy stamps & shoe polish with till the first it will sure get me out of a tight spot. If I was still with the guys I came up here with I could get some from them but we all got separated. Just one colored boy is still with me. Incidentally we left Oklahoma City together but he says he is broke also. This is the thievingest bunch around here I ever saw and all I have to show for it is two extra towels. I haven't heard from anyone since I left Fort Riley. I suppose my letters will catch me someday but it is taking them long enough. This makes the fourth barracks I've moved into since arriving in Belvoir. It seems as if we are moving all the time. How are the kids, all mean as ever? They say that the ones who make the highest scores here get a choice of where they will be shipped next. I mean by that a choice of getting sent to Germany, Alaska, or the far east. I am going to try to be among those high scores. If I'm going overseas I believe I'd rather go to Germany. I've heard so much about it I'd like to see it. Anyhow I want to go somewhere anything to see the different countries. This school lasts eight weeks so I'll be here for a while. I've thought I would get a leave home so often I'm not going to get my hopes too high until I graduate.

Answer soon and tell me all the news.

Tony

Hi Folks [Wilson],

Just a line to let you know I haven't forgotten you. How is everyone ok I hope. Is Doyce still flunking his tests? He should try some of this electricity. Today the captain asked me to stay on here in Belvoir and become a teacher but to do that I would have to stay here at least a month & ½ longer than my eight weeks before getting my leave home. I won't say I'll get to come home after my eight weeks but at least I'll have a chance to before I would if I become a teacher. Possibly I'll be sent overseas after my schooling but if I am it's a chance I'll have to take. As you should know by now a school teacher would not exactly suit me anyhow. I would much rather be out in the air I feel freer. I never knew there were so many words I had never heard of until I came here as much reading as I've done but there are just a whole lot of them used here I've never even dreamed about. Maybe you think these boys with a sixth grade education aren't having trouble. I figure my math and my knowledge of words are why I've done so good so far. Just me and another negro have passed our tests with a high enough score to go to this teacher's school. He took it. I doubt if I'll do as good the rest of the time. We have two books with about as much material in them as they are in one of these pocket books to cover in two weeks. And if I learn all there is to know in them I'll beat what I think I will. After these two weeks we start using what we learned. For three weeks we climb poles and install high lines, then we take up interior installation for three weeks. These last two

"[being] a school teacher would not exactly suit me..."

probably won't come so natural to me. As I can't seem to think of anything else to write guess I'll sign off.

So write soon.

Tony

Hi Folks [Wilson],

How is everyone? Getting as fat as I am? I weigh 185 lbs. now. After receiving all the letters urging me to take this instructors job I investigated and found out I can't now. The captain has already sent the names of the two men chosen to teach. After I told him I wasn't interested in teaching he picked the one with the next highest marks & has already sent in the fact that he wanted them to be transferred to this instructors corps. Also at this time there are people working on my orders that I will receive when I finish this school. That is why I've been trying to enroll in an advanced course in this electricity so soon. If they haven't already got my orders made out by the time I get out of this school I may get to go straight on to the next one. This course is just a sort of ground course. I would like to learn more about it than what I can here. If I don't get the opportunity no one can say I didn't try. I can't hardly get my mind on my writing for these dang people here running around, scuffling, & bumming me for cigarettes & lights. Next week we start working on the poles for three weeks then we take up three weeks interior wiring. We don't work on transformers, rewinding motors, or anything I am really interested in. If I make good on this interior wiring perhaps I'll be able to get a good job while I'm in the army at least even if I don't have

"...I've been trying to enroll in an advanced course in this electricity..."

34

so much of a future in it in civilian life. Speaking of whiskey you know I haven't drank any since I left Fort Riley and very little beer. How is that for improvement? Of course I realize it probably won't last long but here there are so many more things to do than drink and much less expensive. Wanda said something about Doyce[1] quitting school. I hope not. He's been out too much time & money to quit now. Even if he does flunk some of his courses it looks like he would know enough about them to pass them next year. I don't think I explained to mom clearly enough why I couldn't take this job now so show her this.

Write soon

Tony

••

---

1 In addition to building houses, Doyce is a full time student in the Architectural Engineering Program at Oklahoma University.

....

POLE CLIMBING

....

China enters the War; Tony respects the poles

October 29: *The U.N. offensive continues aggressively north of the 38th parallel.*

November 1: *U.S. troops clash with large numbers of Chinese soldiers for the first time.*

For Tony, pole-climbing is tough and scary. He sends money home.

Army training photo

Hi Folks [Burris],

I guess I had better answer your letter before I am disowned. How is everyone these days? Fine I hope. Me I'm about to freeze. It turned cold here about a week ago & I've been shaking ever since. The ground is frozen so hard it hurts my feet to walk on it. I pity these guys who are just starting their pole-climbing. We are on our last week & the poles are already icy at certain hours nearly each morning. They are cutting out these electric courses here. So there will be no other class after we finish because too

"I take my own good easy time..."

many have been getting hurt climbing poles. One boy in our class gaffed out & while sliding down the pole stuck the gaff in his leg & had to have seven stitches in it. I'll bet you'd laugh if you could see me climbing these poles. I take my own good easy time going up them. You know I was never scared of climbing before but since I've been here I've found out just how scary it can be. This class just ahead of us told us how scared they were when they first started climbing. I just laughed at them. I didn't think I would be scared at all but I soon changed my mind. I'm not nearly so scared any more but that first week I certainly was. This is our last week of pole climbing then we start on interior wiring. That should be more interesting. Well it's about school time so I better sign off.

Write Soon

Tony

Dear Mom, Dad, & Kids,

How is everyone fine I hope. I would be doing ok if I didn't have such a cold. Perhaps I can get rid of it now as we've finished with our pole climbing. Next week we start on interior wiring. They say it is pretty easy. If it's as rough as climbing poles I'm afraid I would be very poor at it. You've seen these men climb poles around home it certainly looks easy but you haven't seen them just learning how when they get all the way to the top & gaff out. I gaffed out twice last week but before I hit the ground I gaffed back in. Two of the boys weren't so lucky. One of them threw his arms around the pole & got splinters in his neck. The other one gaffed his ankle. He is still hobbling around from it. I think we graduate about the 1st of Dec. I'll probably be here about a week processing out & waiting on orders. We had a holiday yesterday & guess what I was on K.P. Today I have to serve so I can't go any place. It seems like every time we get a day off I'm on K.P. Well I can't be unlucky all my life. Did you receive my letter? I hope so it had $10 in it. Is Dad still working? How is the car running? Guess I'll close now & go help serve lunch.

Write soon

Tony

Hi B.B.

How are you these days? I dare say not as cold as I am. I guess I'll have to write you first I kept thinking maybe you would write but I guess not. I hear you are getting to be quite a lady's man. Tell all your girlfriends about your handsome brother huh. How is everyone out there? Tell them all hello for me. Are you going home Xmas? If not I may get a leave home around that time & stop over a day or so in Phoenix. I'm getting that old urge to travel again. Eight weeks is too long to be in one place. I sure hope I'm never assigned permanently to any one place. It seems like I just begin to get pretty well acquainted around a place and want to move. Some of the bartenders around hear know me about as well as they did in Chickasha. Are you still picking cotton? Perhaps I'm lazy as hell but that seems like awfully hard work to me. How is your snooker game these days. I'll bet you could beat me now as I haven't shot any since I left home. This is certainly a lazy man's life here. Although we do have to get up early we don't do anything but study for eight hours. I'm gaining weight at it. There is 190 lbs. of me now. Guess I'll close for the time being so tell everyone hello & ans. soon.

Tony

••

Nov. 13, 1950

Howdy Folks [Wilson],

How is everyone in Norman by now? Me I'm freezing. These danged firemen around here don't know how to build a fire. I hear you are planning on moving again. What are you trying to do set a world's record or something? I got up enough energy yesterday to write B.B. a letter. By the time it gets to Arizona he'll probably be back in Oklahoma. You should see me now if you thought I was lazy back home. I'm getting so lazy I have to be begged for a half hour to walk 3 blocks to the show. I guess I'll graduate in three weeks although I won't have as high a grade as I started with. There is a lot of difference in putting on paper what I know & getting up on a pole thirty-five feet in the air & doing it. I still have a fair average but there are several that have better now. I received your letter today but guess I won't get the cookies until tomorrow. If I'm lucky I'll be at home for Christmas. Of course it isn't definite yet but by then I'll have about ten days leave coming & I understand everyone who is here will get ten days off for Xmas. I hope they do that on the post I will be assigned to after I leave here. It couldn't be getting much worse overseas for the paper stated tonight that no more National guards or reserves would be shipped overseas. I wish now I had joined the National guard. They rank up so much faster than the Regular Army.

"If I'm lucky I'll be at home for Christmas."

Tell Burnett if it looks like he is going to be drafted to try to join the national guard. From what I see of them they get a much better deal. For example some of the boys that came from Fort Riley with me are still up in Processing Co. pulling hard labor details. The national guard men were sent up here to go to school & took their place. As long as they keep coming these men will have to stay up there. They have to do their own laundry & everything. Well enough of this as I have to go get some cigarettes.

So answer soon

Tony

••

Nov. 20, 1950

Dear "Bee," Doyce, & "Pete ,"

I guess I'll answer your letter quickly for a change just to surprise you. Besides it's raining and cold outside so I can't go anywhere anyhow. I got a letter from Burnett the other day, he was telling me about all of his girlfriends. I received your cookies & stationery. The cookies were really good & the stationery came in handy for I have to walk about a half mile to the post office to get stamps. It closes at six & the only time I can get off to go up there is from five to six & then I have to rush through chow to make it. I got my billfold back a couple days after it was stolen with all my papers and one dollar in it. A boy claimed he found it in the Latrine and turned it in to the platoon sargeant. I guess he did because he slept on the bottom floor and I slept upstairs at that time. I guess the guy that got it wasn't such a bad guy after all by his leaving a dollar in it. Or perhaps it was so dark he overlooked it. What time did you say Mike's trial comes off? I keep wondering how he will come out. He must be getting wild again there for about six months he wouldn't even drink. Tell everyone at the lumberyard hello for me. I guess I'll close for now as news seems to be awfully scarce.

So write soon,

Tony

....

Hi Folks [Burris],

I will try to answer your letter I received the other day while waiting on my thanksgiving dinner. There does not seem to be much to write about but you get mad if I wait very long to write. How is our football team doing, still winning I hope. We don't get to eat until 1:30. I'll bet you'll are just sitting down to dinner. I hear we will graduate this coming Monday although I'm not sure. They've been throwing this stuff at us so fast I'm getting all mixed up and can't seem to get it all separated. I guess I'll pass without any trouble but I won't have that high mark I was looking forward to. I've been reading a wild western all morning. It certainly is nice to lay up in bed and read for a change. Today the weather is nice out although last night it got down to 15! I guess that's why I keep a cold all the time. This danged weather can't

> "It certainly is nice to lay up in bed and read for a change."

make up it's mind. I guess I'll go to a show this afternoon as I haven't the money to go to town. I have seen more shows in the last month than I saw in a year as a civilian. Well I seem to be running out of news so write soon.

Tony

....

Dear Folks [Burris],

How is everyone? Ok? I sure hated to hear about the battle. If only Lillian hadn't got hurt. What are those poor kids going to do now? I guess there are a lot of people who believe Port beat Dickie up. It sounds very plausible. I know he had it in for Dick. If possible give Lillian my love. Although I gather she is hurt so badly you couldn't see her. Well to talk about something else I finally made pvt. & about time too if you ask me. Did you get my allotment. I hope so as I may get to come home soon. I graduate tomorrow then I'll go to processing company to process out. It will probably take about a week. If I don't get to come home then I will be disappointed again. As I am changing addresses don't write until you hear from me again. I don't know yet what it will be. It's time for the lights to go out so I will close for now.

Tony

....

HOME ON LEAVE

Chinese offensive continues; Tony AWOL

November 25: *The Chinese Army launches a massive attack, along the Ch'ongch'on River, that drives the US Eighth Army out of North Korea. A second attack at Chosin Reservoir on November 27, forces the US X Corp to retreat and fight for survival. This offensive will drive all UN forces out of North Korea by the end of December.*

December 13: *President Truman announces that the U.S. is considering the use of atomic weapons. He declares a state of national emergency on December 15th.*

Tony takes his leave to visit family and friends. He parties hard. A final bender sends him AWOL before he decides to return to the Army.

Chinese troops crossing the Yalu River

Hi Folks [Burris],

Just a line to let you know I haven't forgotten you. I guess you were beginning to wonder when I was going to write. I sure wish I had some of that Oklahoma weather here in my pocket. It has been so long since I've seen weather above freezing I've forgotten how it felt. I guess I'll be at home in about one week and two days from now. Only for about six days tho. I then have to report to Fort Lawton Washington, which is a shipping point for the Far East. I don't guess my signing up for the Far East had a thing to do with this for everyone that is in my graduation class, not assigned to a regular unit, has the same orders. I did a little better in school than I thought. I was fourth from high man in graduating. Of course this may never help me but again it might help me rank up faster when I get with a regular unit. Tell "Bee" and Wanda not to write as I won't be here long enough to receive them. I guess I'll sign off and straighten up my clothes.

Hoping to see you soon,
Tony

Ft. Lawton, Washington
Dec. 25, 1950

Dear "B," "D," & "Pete,"

How are you these dreary days? Oh, that's right though, the sun is probably shining in Okla. I guess you are wondering what is happening to me over my being awol. Well, I've been here about three hours now and as far as I know I may not even be punished. Of course after they get to checking up they may do something but I hardly think so. They told me when I signed in that they hadn't been counting anyone awol if they arrived within five days of the date they were supposed to. I was four days and thirteen hours late so I guess I am still lucky. I don't know now how long it will take me to pay you all I owe but you can bet it will be paid. I want you to know how I appreciate all you've done for me & I guess the only way I can do it is try not to be so much trouble hereafter. I may learn to be a good little boy someday but I doubt it. I'm too ornery to be unlucky, haven't you learned that by now. But you can bet I'll enjoy myself wherever I am. I don't especially like this company I am in now but I don't expect to stay here but a couple days. I process in here and then I guess I'll be moved over to the main post where the rest of my school are. There are only four here I have run into so far but you can't tell when someone else may come dragging in. I was just walking to the chow hall after I arrived and heard someone holler at me. I looked up and there was Adrain Black leaning out a window hollering at me. He's the colored boy I went through basic with if you remember. He and Gibson arrived Saturday so I wasn't so far behind them after all. He said he hadn't done anything but sign in since he arrived so I've caught up with him again. Well I guess I'll close for now. So answer as soon as you get a minute to spare.

"... the sun is probably shining in Okla."

Love,
Tony

....

Dec. 25, 1950

Dear Mom, Dad, & Kids,

I'll drop you a line to let you know I haven't forgotten you. I just arrived about one o'clock. It seems that they allowed us five days absence without counting us awol. So I guess my luck is still holding as I was just four days and thirteen hours late. I am sorry I caused everyone so much worry and trouble but it may be quite a while before I can get on another drunk like the one I was on. I wish now I had stayed at home more while I was there but you know me, can't stay in one place long. I ran into a couple boys that left Fort Belvoir with me in Denver, Colorado. The M.P.s had picked them up then issued them an M.P. pass & meal tickets to get on out here on. I guess this processing co. here is about the rattiest place in the U.S. Army but I'll only be here till I process in then on to another co. Three of the boys I went to school with are still here including the two from Oklahoma I was intending to meet. They only arrived Saturday. So I obviously wasn't the only one who overstayed his leave. I guess I'll have to wear these same O.D.'s until my bag arrives. After waiting on it in St. Louis and in Kansas City I finally checked it straight on here but it hasn't arrived yet. Of course I may have to suffer yet for reporting so late but I hardly think so. I'll find out more about it tomorrow. Well I think I shall close now and try to write "Bee" and Wanda a line. So answer soon.

Love,

Tony

• •

L to R: Dickie Clanton, Jack Stevens, Linard White, Burnett and Tony Burris in front of the Burris home (December 1950).

ABOVE: Burnett, Tony, and Joan Burris (December 1950)

LEFT: L to R: Dickie Clanton, Linard White, Tony Burris in front of the Burris home.

. . . .

KOREA VIA JAPAN

. . . .

U.N. troops retreating; Tony ships out

January 5: *Chinese troops take control of Seoul and continue on the offensive.*

Tony ships out of Fort Lawton. He gets seasick and is not impressed with the cruise ship. Upon arrival, he is also not impressed with Korea.

U.N. soldiers in retreat about 10 miles north of Seoul.

Dear Mom, Dad, & kids,

I write a line so you won't be wondering what's happened to me. I am shipping over in a few hours so you can guess what a turmoil this place is in. I probably won't be able to make sense there is so much racket going on in here. I haven't received any mail since I've been here but I've changed companies three times since arriving so I guess my mail is following me up. I guess you are wondering if they did anything to me for being late. No, they haven't done a thing and won't now. So my luck is holding okay. Have the kids caught the mumps yet? I was thinking about them yesterday and happened to remember they had been exposed to them. Give Wanda and "Bee" my new address as I will not have time to write them today. I guess I had better close and check my clothes once more.

Write soon

Tony

Jan. 11, 1951

Dear Mom, Dad, & Kids,

How is everyone these days? Me, I am ok. I got a little seasick for a while but now I feel natural again. Please, excuse this writing for this boat is rocking up and down all the time. All I've been doing since I got on it, was to pull three hours guard a day. So I have lots of spare time. Everyone says that this is one of the best ships in the Pacific. I'd certainly hate to get on one of the worse ones. We have a movie on board but it is always so crowded I always have to stand up so I seldom ever go. I have been reading these danged pocket books so much that I am actually tired of reading, believe it or not. As, I told you in my last letter I haven't heard from anyone. I guess it will be quite some time before my mail catches me. It will be several more days before we arrive in Japan but I didn't have anything else to do so I thought I'd write even if I can't mail this 'till we arrive. How is the draft situation, does it still look as if it will catch Burnett. I don't know of course but after he becomes reconciled to army life I believe he will like it better than he thinks he will. We all curse it and I would take a discharge any time I could get it but it isn't such a bad life after all. One good thing about it, I don't care what everyone thinks, you can't stay drunk all the time, as I tried to do while I was at home. I guess I'm just a shade homesick but when I wanted to see what this big world looked like I didn't expect to spend all my time looking out a port hole. I guess I am lucky for all my best buddies but one are on this ship who I've met in the army. He is a kid from Texas. He was lucky enough to catch a plane to Japan two days before we left. I expect to see him over there. He graduated from this electrician class with me. I'll sign off for now but will probably write a few more lines before I mail this.

Tony

"... it isn't such a bad life after all..."

....

Camp Drake, Japan
Jan. 19, 1951

Hi Folks [Burris],

Here I am again. I arrived here in Camp Drake, not far from Tokyo, last night about ten. At two fifteen I got in bed, got up at four o'clock and have been out on the rifle range all morning. They say we will not be here over seventy-two hours. The way they are rushing us I believe it. Last night after we got in they checked our shot records, there are over four thousand of us, gave us a partial pay, served us coffee and donuts, issued us bedding, and found out who wanted to make out more allotments. I think I'll make out another twenty-five dollar one for I don't think I'll be spending too much over here. I received a letter from you, Bee, & Wanda yesterday. It was the first I'd heard from any of you. I think I owe "Bee" and Doyce $60 or $70 & Dad I don't know how much I owe him. Make him take one of those checks at least and if you need any more why use them. If it'll make him feel better about it he can surely have made it back by the time I will be needing any of it. Any way find out from Doyce how much I owe him and pay him out of them as soon as possible. I don't believe I thanked anyone properly for the presents they gave me. I was sort of going around in circles I reckon. So if you will tell everyone how much I appreciated their gifts it would please me. Well I'll have to sign off for now but will write again as soon as I get into a regular unit.

"...I don't think I will be spending too much over here..."

Love,

Tony

· ·

Camp Mower, Japan
23 Jan. 1951

Dear Mom, Dad, & Kids,

How is everybody? Fine I hope. Me, Ok, I reckon. They have moved us to three different stations now since I've been here. I am now in Camp Mower but expect to be moved again tonight. We generally get to bed around 12 o'clock and get up about 4:30. The rest of the day we stand in lines waiting on clothing, food, or make out new allotments. I haven't had much time to write and probably

Tony on Fire Guard duty in Japan.

won't have much chance to mail this until tomorrow or the next day but at least I'll get it written perhaps. I've still received only one letter from you but I haven't received any mailed after the sixth of Jan. yet so I guess I have several coming. Perhaps I'll know more about my new address tomorrow. It takes so long for mail to be forwarded from one camp to another I think I'll wait and see if I do get a new address before mailing this. As my time is running out I guess I'll sign off for now. Write often.

Love,
Tony

Wonju, Korea
Jan. 31, 1951

[Tony's letter continues from Korea]

Well here I am in Korea. I am close to a town called Wonju. I understand it is not far from the 38th parallel. I don't believe I would trade one lb. of Okla. soil for all of Korea. I didn't realize these people were so primitive. Don't be alarmed if I don't write often because I seldom ever have the opportunity. Will close for now as one of the men is going in to camp and will mail this for me.

"Well, here I am in Korea."

Love,
Tony

··

HOENGSONG MASSACRE

··

U.N. forces in retreat; Tony survives

February 11: *Massive Chinese attack creates chaos and routs U.N. troops*

Private Tony K. Burris is assigned to the third platoon of L Company, 3rd Battalion, 38th Infantry Regiment of the Second Infantry Division. He "naturally" must help with a bottle of whiskey, then all hell breaks loose.

American soldiers near Hoengsong, February, 1951

Dear Mom, Dad, & All,

I will try to drop you a few as I haven't had time to write recently. I know you worry when I don't write but I have been very busy. I haven't got to bed before twelve and generally am up by three thirty since arriving in Korea. The men over here say the fight against cold weather is the hardest fight of all over here and I can see now why it is. Everyone that has been here for the last two months are very careful with their feet. Most of their feet have been frozen so bad that they are raw and bleeding. The weather is warmer now although I have on three pairs of heavy socks. It gets up around 40° in the day time but the nights are pretty rough. We have rubberized boots that are waterproof but my feet sweat so bad I have to change socks every chance I get. I dry them

"... the fight against cold weather is the hardest..."

out by putting them inside my clothes. I guess you know the Chinese army has disappeared. All we can find are a few North Korean Guerrilla bands and they are pretty scarce. One of the boys I went to school with in Belvoir is still with me. We now operate a #3.5 bazooka. I understand we will be attached to a tank corps today which we will probably be with for a few weeks. One of the boys I went through basic with, whom I slept right under is with our platoon. I was certainly surprised when I saw him. Our company averages one man a day who getting tired of the cold weather shoots himself through the foot which is about the only way they can get out of this cold. It seems to me like they would tough it out for another month when I understand the weather is much warmer. I haven't written Bee or Wanda since I left

Seattle so am going to try to write them a line if my hands don't get too cold. This may be my last opportunity to write for some time to come so if you don't hear from me for a while don't worry. I will write again as soon as I get a chance. Am sending some pictures I had taken in Japan while on fireguard. It was the only chance I had while there to get any taken. Will close now and try to write "Bee" and Wanda.

Love,
T.K.

Dear "Bee, D & Pete,"

I guess this will be a surprise to you it has been so long since I've written but I have been too busy to write. I am now in the 38th Inf. attached to the second division. I guess you know about where we are and have been. We are in a town called Keomsong, I think that's the name of it. It is approximately 33 miles from the 38th parallel. We leave here in a short while sometime today & a rumor is circulating around we are going to Seoul but I don't know for sure yet. I do know our Co. is being attached to a tank corps today to go somewhere. Your fishing box has certainly come in handy. I have all my stationery in it. That is one thing no one has here. I don't know when I'll have to drop it somewhere because of the extra weight but am not going to until I have to. Black and I finally got separated. He is now with some colored outfit. Only two boys are here I knew before, one I went to school with and the other I took basic with. Holt, the boy I went to school with and I are on a bazooka now. They keep trying get us on the machine gun but I want no

"They keep trying to get us on the machine gun but I want no part of it."

part of it. I thought my basic was short but Holt and I are the only ones here who know anything about the bazooka and machine gun too. I guess I'd better close and try to drop Wanda a line before my hands get too cold. My mail still hasn't caught me.

Love,

Tony

Dear Wanda, Virgil & Pam

How is everybody? Me, I am ok when I can stay warm. These Gook house don't seem to be made for warmth. Just a windbreak is about all they are good for. I've just written "Bee" & mom and my hands are sure getting cold. Perhaps you all can compare notes & make a little more out of this. I washed my hands & face for the first time in six days a few minutes ago. It is entirely too cold to worry about being too clean. Our company went on a patrol yesterday and took nineteen North Koreans prisoners without firing a shot. They are about on their last legs it seems. They are cold & hungry as anyone else I guess. We will

"... my hands they are beginning to get numb."

be pulling out of here shortly so I guess I'll make this short. There isn't much to write about besides the cold anyhow. I would certainly enjoy lying down in a nice warm bath tub right now. But I couldn't change clothes even if I could find a bathtub everything I have now I'm wearing besides socks. I guess I'll close & go warm my hands they are beginning to get numb. Write when you can for it may be some time before I get another chance to write you.

Love,

Tony

Dear Mom, Dad, & Kids,

I suppose you will have heard before you receive this that I have been wounded in action. I know you will be worried but I can't even bum a stamp around here so far to mail a letter. Here in Japan we have to have stamps you know. It will be the 23rd before I receive any pay but am going to write anyhow, perhaps I can beat some of the people out of a stamp. Do not worry about me as I am alright. I just got a little bitty bullet in the fleshy part of my leg. I can't even get these people to take it out for me. We were almost due north of Wonju about thirteen miles from the 38th parallel the 11th of February when we first got attacked.

We had been running into small arms fire for several days when the afternoon of the 11th about dark mortar shells started dropping around us. We only had two squads of men besides the South Koreans and tank's crew. We drew back about six miles and joined the rest of our company and a company of artillerymen. I was second on guard so I didn't go to bed until I had pulled my shift. As I came off guard I found our squad leader had a fifth of whisky & as I was the only one awake it seemed I just naturally had to help him drink it but just then they hit us again. Everything was in confusion. The South Koreans kept running in between me and my squad & I got lost from them. We had been retreating down the road and I saw what looked like everybody abandoning the road and vehicles. I ran along with them and I guess I fought my way along a creek for two hours and then decided most of the Americans were back on the road. I went back but never was able to find my squad.

Nearly daylight we seemed to get our worst attack. I

think that was when our squad was hit the hardest. Bugles started blowing & although there was an occasional bullet flew over me the main attack was a couple blocks up the road. I had fallen in the creek and lost my bedroll & stuff but I had taken the bible Bee gave me with her and Joe's picture in it out that day & was showing them to the boys. I had stuck them in my pocket & still have them.

My feet were about to freeze when we finally got to move again at daylight. I bummed rides in trucks, jeeps, & tanks until I decided there were more bullets aimed at them than at the infantry. I joined Hqts. Co. of some outfit I don't know what & fought our way on through until about seven o'clock P.M. the 12th. We were almost through them and I was congratulating myself on not getting a scratch & running alongside the road when it seemed like a rock flew up & hit my leg. I kept running. About fifty feet further on I felt blood running down my leg.

"My feet were about to freeze when we finally got to move ... at daylight."

I knew then I had been shot but it still didn't hurt. I guess I ran alongside the vehicles 2½ or 3 miles more before I got afraid I'd lose enough blood to pass out. I had seen so many fall and no one stop to see about them that this worried me. Nearly all the vehicles were loaded but by standing on one leg & leaning over another wounded man I found room on a tank. By this time we were about through them anyway so I wasn't so scared of my exposed position.

They took us to a medical station where I saw one of the men in our squad. He said so far as he could find out he was the only one not hit. The day before he had found out our squad leader was shot through the foot but didn't know for sure whether he or anyone else had gotten out. As far as I know today he & I were the only ones out of nine men who got out alive[1]. Incidentally he didn't know what had happened to that fifth of whiskey.

To show what cowards the South Koreans are I'll relate a little incident I witnessed about six the twelfth. This is just one such happening. We had found out several hours before that we had to fight our way out if we were going to get out. Myself, about ten Koreans & two other G.I.'s whose companies had been shot to pieces were going to take a hill alongside the road to let the vehicles through. The Koreans had found out they would have to help fight if they still had rifles & ammunition. I had just crossed a gully & was leading the men up the hill. The other two G.I.'s were behind these Koreans to make sure they went up the hill and did not turn back as they had been doing. I looked behind me in this gully and this Korean had grabbed his M-1 by the muzzle & was beating the stock against the ground trying to break it so he wouldn't be forced to go. Just as the stock of the rifle broke the weapon went off and shot him. Where I don't know and don't care. I should have left him there but he was crying & yelling so I finally decided to get him back on the road. So I made two other Koreans help him. Anyway we went ahead and took the hill without him & his two friends who were pleased to get back to the road themselves. I don't blame them for being afraid but I do blame them for not fighting after seeing we had to fight to get out.

Shortly after this we were on another hill. I guess I was more frightened in this incident than at any time. We had instructions to take this hill and hold it until three tanks that had come in could get turned around and start back leading our whole line of vehicles. I was again ahead of the

---

1 This battle became known as the Hoengsong Massacre: both sides suffered tremendous casualties as the U.N. forces were eventually able to hold and counterattack.

rest of the men. Perhaps ten feet higher than anyone else on the hill. I was straining every nerve listening for signs of the enemy coming up the hill & wishing the tanks weren't so slow about getting turned around. Finally the last one got turned around and I turned around myself to start toward them. I immediately saw I was alone on the hill. I still do not know when the rest of the men had pulled out but you can bet I was traveling at top speed all the way to the road about ½ mile.

> "I sure wish I could stay in one place long enough to get my mail..."

After that we all stuck close to the road until we got out. I guess we had traveled about 1 mile when I got hit. After that I traveled by tank, trucks, planes, or any way I could to get here. I don't think I'll be here much longer, not over a month at the most. I'll be sent back to my old outfit. I sure wish I could stay in one place long enough to get my mail. I still haven't heard from anyone since I left Japan the last time. I will mail this as soon as I can beat someone out of a stamp. I seem to have run out of anything to say so I will close for now. Tell everyone hello for me.

Love,

Tony

....

Camp Nara, Japan
25 Feb. 1951

Dear Mom, Dad, & All,

Just a line to let you know I'm still alright and have changed addresses again. I am now in a camp called Nara. It is supposed to be a rest camp for us poor old wounded veterans. Ha!

They are trying to get us back in condition to go back to Korea. When I arrived here they told me I would probably be here for two weeks but I think I can keep these doctors guessing about my leg for three at least. I am supposed to be taking light exercises now but I'm not any sorer than some of the men on full exercise. I guess you'll think I'm just lazy but if I can stay in Japan until the weather in Korea gets warm I'll be that much better off. The tips of my fingers and toes still tingle from my few days over there as is. If I had stayed over there all this time I expect I would be starting back to the states by now with frostbitten hands & feet. Does Linard's folks ever hear from him? I would like to know what outfit he's with. It's beginning to look like my letters will never catch me to find out though. I still haven't heard from anyone. I can't figure out how the government keeps up with me I move around so much.

"The tips of my fingers and toes still tingle [from frostbite in Korea]..."

I shot pool all day yesterday. It seemed about like old times in the Blanchard Pool hall. My feet were certainly tired when I went to bed last night. I am sitting here now trying to write this letter and sweat a pool game. Pool is about the only free recreation here now and I don't get paid until tomorrow. I've been bumming cigarettes from the Red Cross since I got hit. In Korea they come in our rations. I think I'll close and get in this pool game. Ha!

Love,

Tony

••

··

REHAB

··

U.N. troops take the offensive; Tony recovering

March 18: *U.N. troops recapture Seoul.*

Tony is in rehab at Camp Nara, Japan. He has time to think about the war, family, and friends. He receives letters mailed in January.

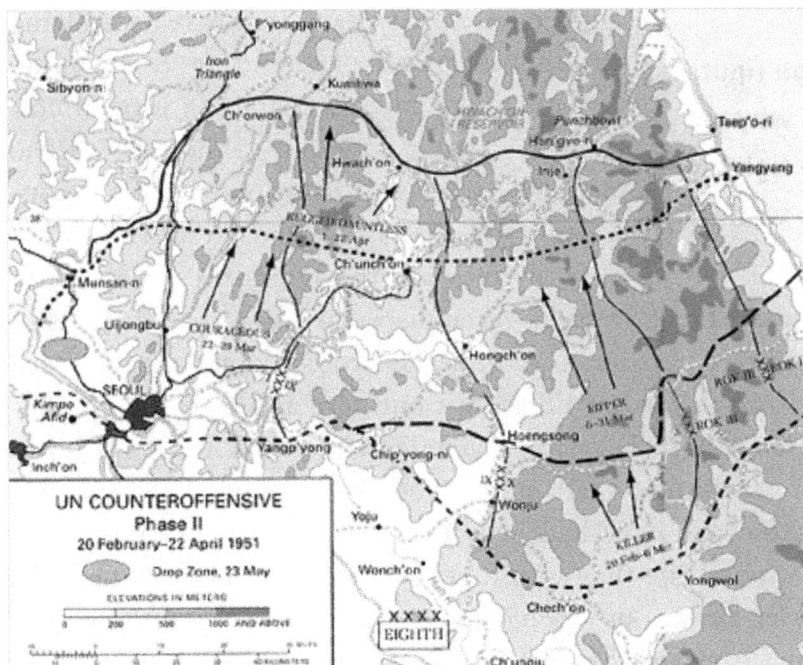

Korean Battles 1951

Dear "Bee, Dee, & Pete,"

I've just received your letter of January 21st. I received one from mom with it and yesterday I received a letter from Wanda and a radiogram from mom, but I guess you know all about this radiogram. Anyway I am catching up on the news in January. I expect I'll be leaving here in ten days or somewhere around that date anyway. When I leave here I'll get seven days furlough to rest up. Ha! I guess Doyce will be getting his vacation soon. Is he going to build more houses? I've been letting on to these doctors my leg was troubling me but I guess I didn't do such a good job of acting today or else they've been spying on me anyway they put me on full exercise today dang it. There I was lying around about all day reading & sleeping, shooting pool and just loafing in general now I am back to a poor old soldiers life. Road marches, exercises, formations, and what nots. I could get a pass now and go into town but it is always dark the hours these passes are given, there are only three places in Nara not off-limits to military personnel, & these Jap women don't appeal to me either so I guess I'll stick it out here and save what money I have until I get my seven day leave then I can see Japan in daylight & tell more about it perhaps. The last four shows we have had here I've already seen in Ft. Belvoir. It looks like they would get some new shows for the G.I.s over here. Can you figure out why we are fighting this war and what good it is doing? I've done considerable thinking on it recently and I can't see any sense to it. I've heard all the arguments about the communists and all that but we are losing so much equipment over there I cannot see any

"Can you figure out why we are fighting this war...?"

material gain. Someone will probably say, "But the Reds are losing equipment too." They aren't or at least they don't have hardly any. I've seen Chinese lined four deep. The first man in line had a rifle when he is shot down the man behind him picks it up and comes on and so on down the line. As a rule these rifles are American M-1's they have picked up so how can they be losing anything but their lives. Guess I'll close as I am running out of space.

Write often,

T.K.

....

March 6 – 1951

Dear Wanda, Virgil, & Pam

I received your letter dated January 17th just yesterday and decided to answer it. Although it has followed me from Camp Drake and Camp Mower all over Korea and thru three different hospitals it and a radiogram I received yesterday from mom are the first news I've had from home since I left Camp Drake the twentieth of January. I am in now what is called a rest camp in Nara, Japan. The two weeks I have been here I've been on limited exercise but today I was put on full exercise so I guess I'll have to go back to work. While I was on limited exercise I got up at 5:30 had until 8:00 to go to work & then we would go to a movie & have one hour in the gym to play basketball in and off the rest of the day. I've been reading and shooting pool almost all that time. I just answered mail call and received a letter each from mom & "Bee", both dated in January so my mail is finally catching me. So Burnett went to California eh? He's getting to be quite a rambler. Did I tell you about the time Burnett & I were in the city, while I was home

"I am in now what they call a rest camp in Nara, Japan..."

65

on furlough, he and Connel Roberts has sat down across the room from us with a couple women. They seemed to be getting along alright so Burnett calls me back to the restroom & asks me if I wanted him to introduce me to his new friend. We had been up all night before and he was so tired and sleepy he just couldn't stay up longer so he was going home and wanted to fix me up with his girlfriend. Anyhow I was otherwise occupied right then and couldn't so he went on home. Every time I think about that I get a big laugh. As I can't seem to think of anything else to write will close for now. If I don't write as often as I should forgive me for you know how I hate to write.

Love,
Tony

••

March 10

Dear Mom, Dad, & Kids,

How are you these days? Me, I'm as healthy as ever. I leave here Monday or Tuesday to Camp Drake. I'll be there a week or more I guess. I have received a couple letters & a package from you up to date. I was tickled to get the package but somehow the letters seemed more important. Perhaps it is because I can get candy and stuff here easily. We haven't had mail call yet today. I should get a letter from Bee & Doyce according to your letter. It has been rain here for the last twenty-four hours or so which sure makes me feel closed in. It is a chilly rain and the chill seems to have got inside the building. I was glad to get Jo & Karen's letters. Right now any news from home is certainly welcome. I guess I'm just homesick, anyway as far as I'm concerned these Orientals can keep these countries as I have

"I guess I'm just homesick..."

come to the conclusion I like the "States" better. How is Lillian Clanton doing she hasn't been mentioned by anyone as yet. Well guess I'll close as news is awfully scarce here.

Write often,

Tony

Dear Mom, Dad, & all,

Just a line or two to let you know I am alright & where I am. I am now back in Korea. Tomorrow or the next day I will rejoin my company. My trouble with my stomach has been bothering me some recently. The doctor in Nara said it was my kidneys. Perhaps it will get serious enough for me to go back to Japan but I have my doubts. I guess I'll have to wait a couple more months to receive any mail but keep sending it as I enjoy it when it does catch me. I hardly know what to write about as news seems awfully scarce. I probably won't write very often until I get settled. If when I catch it our company is on the move I won't have much opportunity. I will be glad in a way to catch them as I am not in very good physical condition. There I'll get enough exercise to get back in shape quick. Well guess I'll close so keep writing.

T.K.

"I am now back in Korea."

BACK IN ACTION

Truman fires MacArthur; Tony not in shape

April 11: *President Truman replaces MacArthur with Gen. Matthew Ridgeway.*

Tony is back with his company. His friends are mostly gone. Later he credits the Chinese with a better foxhole design.

Foxholes

Dear Mom, Dad, & All

I'll try to write a line or two while I have the opportunity. I am sitting up here on top a mountain about 6 miles from the thirty-eight parallel. We've been going on patrols every day nearly since I got back so I haven't had much opportunity to write. I haven't even been able to get close enough to civilization to receive my mail. One day we did get mail, I received three letters from "Bee" written in February so I know I'll

"[My feet] have been lightly frost-bitten..."

have quite a bit of mail if I ever do catch that mail man. The weather is a wee bit warmer now although it snowed a couple nights ago. I'm sitting here waiting on chow to arrive as I still have a good appetite. My feet and legs have certainly been sore since I got back. Not having done much walking while in Japan I had to get used to it all over again. I've about walked the stiffness out of my legs but I'm afraid it will be quite a while before my feet quit hurting. They've been lightly frost-bitten and don't get over that very quickly over these rocky hills. I guess I'll sign off for now as I can't think of anything to write. Keep writing often as I'll enjoy my mail when I do get it.

Love, *T.K.*

Dear Witts,

Surprised huh? I just received three letters from you & have about ½ hour's leisure so will try to write you, I'll drop "Bee" a line when I get her new address for I know how I hate for my mail to follow me from one place to another. No, I never received your package although I may yet. I've received two from "Bee" & one from Mom. I got a letter from Thomas the other day. He is in Puson & I've been there three times and didn't know it. You asked if I wanted anything. Food is always welcome to me ha I need another lead pencil but by all means don't send an expensive one for I'll just lose

"I even got to take a shower the other day."

it. No, I haven't seen anyone I know as yet but I am now assistant squad leader. I was put in for P.F.C. a couple days ago but it may be two months before it becomes official. We are now in reserve, behind the 23rd Inf. having rifle inspection & shaving every day. I even got to take a shower the other day. I don't know how long we'll be back here but I hope a couple weeks at least. I just received a letter from "Bee" so I guess I'd better answer it. It has been nice weather here up to a couple hours ago. Now it is raining and sleeting & these ponchos don't make as good a tent as shelter-halves do. I guess I'd better close as I'm running out of space.

Keep Writing To

T. K.

· ·

April 11, '51

Dear "Bee", Doyce, & Larry,

I will try to answer your letter which I just received. It was written April 1. I guess that is about the fastest mail travels up here. As for my physical condition I was awfully short winded when I first got back. Laying around hospitals for a month & ½ gets a person out of shape. For three or four days I certainly lagged behind on these hills but am ok now. There aren't but three or four guys left in the company that I knew. It seems a large part of the company was captured by the Chinese in that Hoensong roadblock, perhaps you heard about it in the news, where I was wounded. A lot of them have been recovered but they get to the States after being captured. The chinks take one of their dogtags & if they recapture them they kill them. They say they are treated nice by the Chinese. They feed them good & do not torture them like the North Korean. We are now in Battalion Reserve. If the 23rd doesn't have too much trouble we will get to stay for a few weeks. My hands were slightly frostbitten but not as bad as my feet. My writing would be much better if I had a decent place to write. I'm writing this on back of a canteen cup. Yes, I received your 2 packages, one in the hospital and one a couple days ago. Everyone really liked your fruit cake & I'll have to admit I liked that Chili. It was really good for a change. As it's getting dark & I'm getting awfully cramped in this position I don't guess I'll write Mom. Tell her I'll write the next chance I get which should be tomorrow unless we catch a patrol.

Love,

T.K.

* *

April 15, 1951

Hi Folks [Burris],

I'm sorry I haven't written sooner but since we've been in reserve I've been busier than when on the line it seems. I am starting this in my noon hour. I don't know when I'll get to finish it. For the last four or five days we've been getting up at five-thirty having classes on different kinds of weapons & taking exercises after dark. I don't have light to write by & am as a rule too lazy. The weather is warming up pretty good now. I received thirteen letters yesterday & the day before I got a box of candy from "Bee". So I guess I'm doing all right by my mail now. If that old watch is still running I could certainly use it now. It only took "Bee's" box about nine days to get to me so I guess it would be safe to send it.

Is Jack Stephens in the service yet. I don't ever hear anything about him anymore. It is now six-thirty and almost dark so I'll try to get this finished. I might take in the show at seven-thirty. It is set up here in the open. There is a band here also. The show isn't too plain if the night is light but it is a change.

I could make a rank fast if my leg would hold up but on an extra-long hike it stiffens up on me and I can't keep up with the best hikers. I can stay up with some but I can't keep up with our lieutenant and he has noticed it. He seems to like me but he believes a man with rank should be able to stay ahead of everyone else so I don't guess I'll rate up fast under him. I'm sure I could have if it wasn't for my leg. Well I'll sign off for now so keep writing.

Love,
T.K.

··

April 17, 1951

To Mom,

Just a line tonight to let you know I have not forgotten you. Tomorrow we go on a three or four day patrol so I'd better mail this now. I understand all the territory we cover on this patrol is behind the front lines and has been patrolled recently but we have made the mistake several times before of letting enemy soldiers infiltrate behind the lines, so we are trying to keep the area behind the lines clear now so don't worry. Perhaps I'll have more time to write when I return. I guess I'll sign off now as we get up at four thirty in the morning.

Here's wishing you a very happy birthday and mother's day. Love,
T.K.

April 17, 1945

Dear Mom,

Just a line tonight to let you know I have not forgotten you. Tomorrow we go on a three or four day patrol so I'd better mail this now. I understand all the territory we cover on this patrol is behind the front lines and has been patrolled recently but we have made the mistake several times before of letting enemy soldiers infiltrate behind the lines, so we are trying to keep the area behind the lines clear now so don't worry. Perhaps

I'll have more time to write when I return. I guess I'll sign off now as we get up at four thirty in the morning.

Here's wishing you a very happy birthday and mothers day.

Love,
T. H.

Dear Folks [Burris],

Well here I am again back in reserve again as I told you I might be. On our three day patrol we ran up against no opposition at all. I've been shining my mess gear for the past two hours. We have a new regimental commander and he is going to hold an inspection here of all places. My hands are black from being dirty so long and chapped from exposure to the weather but my mess gear shines like a new dollar. I understand we are even going to shine our boots tomorrow but where we'll get the time and polish I don't know.

How is B.B.'s draft trouble coming along? I'd hate to see him get sent over here, as he might not be able to hide and run as fast as I can. I guess he's about as big as I am now though. I don't know for sure but I'll bet I don't weigh over 170. I believe running over these hills would keep anyone lean. We've climbed hills, with our bedrolls, that I believe would make a mountain goat ashamed of himself. We've

"My hands are black from being dirty so long and chapped..."

been going down in the villages back in the hills picking up all the Koreans of military age around here. You'd be surprised how many we do find. If they get tired of the ROK Army they slip off into the hills and hide out. I got a letter from Dickie today.

It seems he saw my address in the *Blanchard News* while I was in the hospital. I couldn't read half of it. I guess I'll have to give him a lesson in writing. Well guess I'll close for now & get some sleep.

Write often

T.K.

Dear Mom, Dad, & All,

I'll try to write a line or two tonight although I hardly know what to write about. I've just finished polishing my boots of all things to do but the army refuses to let anyone sit around over here it seems.

Our old platoon sargeant just got back from the hospital, our former acting platoon sargeant is now my squad leader, my former squad leader is now assistant squad leader, & I've been reduced to second scout. I suppose by the time you receive this letter it won't be news anyhow so I may as well tell you we have received word that our Dday & Hhour has been decided on. I don't know when it is of course but I don't think they would have told us if it wasn't soon. It seems the Chinks have decided to launch a new offensive too which may mess up the plans for our offensive moves. I personally believe the U.N. is going to try one big push to end this war before many of the older veterans of this war are rotated.

Of course that is just a wild guess but I hope it hits the truth for if everyone in this company that has had over six months in Korea is rotated I'll be about the oldest man in the company & I know I don't know enough about the Chinese tactics to feel secure yet. I haven't received my mail in the last couple days. It's certainly been disappointing but will probably receive quite a bit again when I do. Well guess I'll close for now so write often & let Wanda & "Bee" know I wrote as I'm tired & lazy & don't think I'll write them tonight.

Love to all

Tony

Dear "Bee, D & Pete",

I guess I'll try to write a line or two although I hardly know what to write about. Two of the men who were in my squad before I got wounded are now back with the company. One of them a long-legged Texan about my size is now in the same squad again and we are sharing a pup tent. I received word from a pretty reliable source the other day that no one from our regiment will be rotated until this new Chinese attack is over with, so that will be just that much longer before it becomes my turn. Of course there aren't many left in the 38th Regiment that came over with them but they all get first chance which is only right. Perhaps by July or September they will all be rotated & I'll get my chance. I'd certainly hate to spend another winter here. It is still so chilly at nights I've quit going to the show. It has quit being fun to watch a movie in the damp air. Well I'll close this and write again when I get the energy & have a better pencil.

Write Often, to

Tony

• •

April 26

Dear Mom,

It is now 3 P.M. & we shove off at 4. I thought I'd drop you a line before we go. I am in the 3rd Bn. in case you hear anything about us on the news. I don't suppose I'll have time to write or a chance to mail it if I do for several days so you'll understand why you don't receive any letters. We are relieving the 23rd Reg. which has been flanked on both sides by enemy. I don't have time to write more now so I'll write as soon as possible. I wrote Bee earlier today before we knew we were moving. Tell everyone Hello for me,

    T.K.

29 April, 1951

Dear Witts,

    How is everybody? Me I'm up here on a hill taking a sunbath. The last two days it has been raining a little so this sun sure feels good. I have my shirt & boots off & boy does it feel good. At night I'm pretty careful about keeping my boots on as I've talked to a few people who swear that it isn't any fun to run over these sharp rocks at night barefooted. I don't know how long it will

> **"You should see the foxhole I've just dug."**

be before I can mail this but I will soon as I catch someone going back to the rear. You should see the foxhole I've just dug. It's about seven feet long 3 feet wide and 3 feet deep. On each end we have about a foot and a half that we keep open. In the center we have about eight inches of dirt to protect us from mortars. A lesson we learned from "Joe Chink." Eight inches of dirt will pretty well stop a morter & 1½ foot opening is rather hard to hit. How is B.B's draft situation coming? I hope he doesn't pass the physical. Well guess I'll sign off & let another fellow use this writing material. As I am not writing mom today let her know I wrote.

    Tony

....

INJE AND CHUN-CHON

....

Chinese attack and UN counterattack; Tony is exhausted

May 15: *Chinese begin their second spring offensive.*

May 20: *the U.N counter offensive drives them back over the next twenty days with tremendous losses on both sides.*

Tony does some landscaping. He is afraid to make new friends because of casualty rates. The platoon is exhausted by the end of the month, but Tony must fight again on May 30, his 22nd birthday. Borbon helps Tony get their men out of an ambush.

Tony (r) and friends cleared timber around their foxhole.

Dear Folks [Burris],

Here I am again after so long a time. I have been too busy to do much writing recently but will try to write a line or two. There is so little to write about over here. The same old thing nearly every day. Up at daylight, a long march or dig a foxhole & clear timber out from in front of it for a half mile then when dark arrives pull guard half the night. If a flare is set off or someone gets nervous & lets loose a shot I pull guard all night. I'm sure glad I don't require as much sleep as lots of people for this gets rough. Of course I can stand this a long time before having people shooting at me but it still hard to take sometimes. I received the watch a couple days ago, pretty fast, huh. There is a rumor going around that we go back in reserve the tenth. That's the kind of rumor I love to hear come true.

These guard hours up here are about twice as long as they are back behind the lines. The other night someone got nervous about nine o'clock & shot up a clip of M-1 ammunition. It was a very dark night & I lay there straining my eyes and ears the rest of the night. Along about 3 o'clock my eyes started playing tricks on me. Small bushes and brush piles got up and started running all over the hillside in front of me.

"Small bushes ... got up and started running all over the hillside..."

A little more & I would have been burning up ammunition. Anyway just at daylight I got my hatchet & go down & cut those bushes down & carried them further down the hill.

We now have a big brush pile all the way in front of our position. I don't think any person could get through without making a lot of racket. I guess I'll close this & write again when I have more time. So keep writing & I will answer when I can. Love to all,

T.K.

....

Dear Mom,

I finally have time to drop a line, as you know by now I suppose we have been very busy. Of the 48 men in our platoon who came out of reserve with me the 26th of April there are fifteen left. We fought Chinese in the central area around Chun-Chon & when every other division had retreated we fought our way out & started on a new offensive towards Inje. We are about a day & ½ from Inje now with paratroopers in Inje. So maybe tomorrow or the next we will get to go back to reserve. I'm tired and know everyone else is. We've worked day & night under a strain so long that I just can't go much further. I'll bet I don't weigh over 160 lbs. now but I'm still alive so I can't complain. I'm afraid to like anyone over here much now I've lost so many good friends.

"I'm afraid to like anyone over here much now I've lost so many good friends."

I received Wanda's package just now. We've been traveling the hills so long all they would bring us were letters. They had to burn some of our mail when we pulled off that last hill. As usual I left everything back there but my ammunition and rifle.

I am now in command of fifteen men. You might say sort of assistant platoon sargeant. I made P.F.C. the fifth of May & am in for Cpl. but possibly will not get Cpl. rating for a while as I have been P.F.C. such a short time. If I do though the Platoon Sgt. says I'll be put in for S. Sgt. immediately. I'm not too interested in making Sgt. though as I hope to get sent to the States soon & I couldn't hold a sgt. rating now as I know so little about army regulations.

I am going to close for now as I want to try to rest enough where I can go tomorrow, my birthday. I hope it will be my last day on the line for a long time. Give "Bee" & Wanda a ring as I am just writing you.

Love

T.K.

4 June, 1951

Dear Mom, Dad, & All

I think I'm going to have time to write for a change so will try to write a line or two. Nothing has happened much for the last few days. We are still close to the lines but are not fighting now. Our former platoon sargeant, who is now a first sargeant, just told me we go back into corps reserve tomorrow so I guess we might make it this time. I keep hoping the whole division will get back in army reserve before long. We haven't been in army reserve yet and I understand when we do it will last about a month and one half. By that time I would have my six months in and possibly get back to the states for a while. Of course there are still a lot of old men here that have been here for over six months but possibly this rotation will speed up a lot in the next month & a half, let's hope so. We were in a little road block a week ago or rather on my birthday. I was lucky. I brought all seventeen of our men out without a scratch. I had to chase some of them out from under rocks and nearly beat up on some to keep them moving but we made it. Every other platoon had casualties in it but I have a good assistant, a little Spanish boy named Borbon, who has all kinds of guts and between us we made them move. If I had got in a condition like that a month ago I couldn't have done it. I was in too poor physical condition. If B.B. does get in the army be sure to stress to him to get in good condition and stay that way for it will probably save his life at some time or other if he comes over here. I guess I'll sign off for now as I've about run out of words so I guess I'll close. Have you heard anything about La Vern Peters. He should be home very soon it seems to me like. Write often.

    T.K.

5 June, 1951

Dear "Bee, D & Pete",

    A line to let you know I haven't forgotten you. You know, I see by the letter I received from you a couple days ago, what we have been doing since the 26th of April. I only had time off up til now to write Mom more than two or three letters during that time. We are still in Inje but the other U.N. troops have moved on north so there is no fighting going on here now. I hear we are just waiting for orders to go into reserve for a while. It is certainly about time. We have gotten in a few replacements but no one as yet that has seen any combat. I wish they would give us some squad leaders that are veterans in this war as I would like to give my job away. I don't exactly enjoy having people's lives depending on my decisions & besides if I was still just a rifleman I could protect my own life a little better. We still have some men who came over last August with the 38th Reg. so I guess I'll be over here some time yet. There doesn't seem to be a thing I can write about so I guess I'll close this. By the way did anyone have my address put in an Arizona paper? I received a letter from a girl in Buckeye yesterday that had been mailed to me while I was in the hospital. So naturally I'll have to write her and find out just what kind of person she is. A lot of my mail was destroyed when we finally had to pull out of the central front so there was quite a gap in there where I didn't receive any. I received your birthday card yesterday and threatened to hang it on the wall of my tent but each morning we have to roll them up. Excuse the writing as I am in a very uncomfortable position. Write often.

Tony

· ·

6 June, 1951

Dear Witts,

I'll try to write a line before dark. How is everybody these days. Me, I'm alright. Still sweating out reserve. We haven't seen any action since May 30 but we are still too close to the front lines to suit me. I received two packages from you since I've written last but I'm pretty sure the other was lost when we were surrounded on the central front. I understand there was a lot of mail just came in the night before we had to pull out. I guess "Joe" Chink had a good time eating my box. I received your letter written 29 May a while ago. Did the folks make it up on my birthday. I didn't exactly enjoy my birthday. We started the morning off by wading a river. Then it started raining and we got drenched. Then we were caught in a roadblock & were forced to retreat so all in all it was an unsuccessful day. We had a traveling stage show today. A sort of musical, I really enjoyed it. It's been so long since I've heard any music I guess you might say I am starved of it. I hate to think what I would be like if I'd been over here for ten months like some G.I.s. Well guess I'll close I seem to have run out of words. There just isn't anything over here I care to write about so guess I'll sign off for now.

Love,

T. K.

"We are still too close to the front lines to suit me..."

· ·

THE LULL

Peace talks begin; Tony in reserve

July 8, 1951: *Armistice talks begin at Kaesong.*

Tony has more rank and responsibility. He takes pride in the squad he and Borbon have trained, and he values the handkerchiefs and Tabasco from home. His father Sid has written a letter complaining about the lack of recent letters from Tony.

Now in reserve, Tony has time to think and write about the peace negotiations. He would just as soon "drop matters as they stand," and two wasted years later negotiators reach the same conclusion. Rotation remains elusive.

11 June, 1951

Dear Mom,

Just a few lines tonight before I go to bed. I am back in reserve again in the east central sector, which is our old stomping grounds, so I feel more at home. I know this country pretty good in through here now, I've been over it so much. I'm Sargeant of the Guard tonight so I don't guess I'll get too much sleep. They give me all the duties of a sargeant but I only get paid for a P.F.C. I won't complain though if I get out of here in a short time which I am sure

> "I am... back in our old stomping grounds, so I feel much more at home."

hoping for. I probably couldn't hold a sargeant's rating after I get to the States anyway as I don't know much about the army as yet. Just the short period of basic train is all the real training I've had. It seems funny but I've really learned little or nothing while in actual combat that will help me when I get back to army life in the States. A heck of an Army, huh, I'll have to admit it is the best though. Even though some of the other countries may have better individual fighters we have a far superior army. Well I guess I'd better sign off for now. Write often & if you wish & can send me a box of canned foods like chili & tamales & maybe a small bottle of pepper sauce or Tobasco sauce.

Love to All,

T.K.

Dear Folks [Burris],

Just a few lines tonight to let you know I am alright & give you an idea of what I've been doing. We are in Corps reserve close to the area we were in reserve in April near Chun-chon. We get up each morning at five-thirty for reveille just like garrison in the States. After reveille we eat & shave & at 7:30 police up all the trash in the company area. At eight we fall out for bayonet drill, at eight-thirty close order drill, and today we were digging positions like we made last month on what we call "bunker hill". Our Battalion is famous for its defense there. Of the evenings we play ball of some sort as a rule. After the rest of the men get off at five, I have to attend an N.C.O. meeting & then teach one of my men the manual of arms and what I think he should know about the M-1. He was in the Air Corps before & they drafted him in the army. He has never had any training on the M-1 at all. He can't even take it apart. One day's training he had before he left the States. I am now a big corporal. Ha. One month and ten days a P.F.C. Pretty quick eh. If they will send me back to the States I'll give them these two stripes right quick if they want them. Write soon & tell me all the news as I haven't heard from anyone for three days.

Love to All,
T.K.

"If they will send me back to the States I'll give them these two stripes right quick...

Tony's father, Sid Burris, received the following letter from Lieutenant Carse.

17 June 51,
Korea

Dear Sir,

Received your letter dated 9 June 51 in regard to your Son not writing home.

Your Son, Cpl. Tony K. Burris is a member of my company and in the best of health.

I talked to your Son and he claims he has been writing home the last few weeks however there was a period when we were very busy and unable to write. Your Son is a fine boy and doing a very good job.

Sincerely,
Roy A Carse
1st Lt. Inf,
Commanding, Co. L

18 June 51

Dear "Bee, D & Pete",

I'll try to drop a line or two tonight although there isn't really much to write about. I received a letter from Mom today and she had just received a letter from me, the first since May 6. I must have gotten a letter lost somewhere because I wrote her about May 18th. I received your package today & was really glad to get it. I sure appreciate Larry's gift & thank him very much. The bible is nice and I am glad to have it but somehow I've grown attached to the old one so will try to keep the two of them. As for the handkerchiefs, this is the first time I've had anything to blow my nose on in about two months, besides my sleeve. My old squad leader got back yesterday and has taken over another squad.

87

I wanted him to take mine but the platoon sargeant decided to give him the other. I have some good men in my squad and hope I've learned enough and can teach them enough to insure their safe return to their homes. I have only seen one squad over here I thought was better, my former squad in May, and I hope to make this squad as good before we see combat. With the help of my assistant squad leader, Borbon, who was in my squad before & my BAR man who was in the same platoon, I believe I can. I'll close for now as I can't seem to write a long letter any more. Write often,

To *T.K.*

23 June '51

Dear Mom, Dad, & Kids,

Just a line to let you know I'm still alright. We had an inspection today by Major General Ruffner Second Division Commander. He seems to be very proud of his division which he well should be. There isn't much to write about so this will probably be a very short letter. We are still in Corps Reserve and hoping to go into Army Reserve. If we could I would probably have more than my six months in over here and might get out. We train all the time in reserve but it isn't as hard on a man as fighting is so I'm not complaining. I wish I had gotten some of this training in the States. I think everyone should to get in condition if for no other reason. Well guess I'll sign off and go to bed.

Love,

T.K.

1st July, 1951

Dear Mom, Dad, & Kids,

Just a line to let you know I am alright. We are still in Corps Reserve & listening very closely to these cease fire rumors. I haven't heard from you for a couple days but have been getting letters from "Bee" and Wanda & one from Karen. The fourth day of this month will make six months since I left the States. The 26th will make one year I've been in the army. Six months over here and almost six months in the States since I joined. I've seen a lot of miles, quite a few of them on foot, since I enlisted. I'm going to try to get in something besides the infantry when I get back as I'm tired of walking. How is everybody. Wanda tells me I have a new cousin. *Did someone put my name* in the paper in Arizona when I was in the hospital? I received a letter from a young lady out there who said she got my address from the newspaper. If you can believe pictures she is really nice looking but the world seems to have several of them although I haven't seen any running around loose over here. I guess T.D. and Perry will start to school this fall. I sure don't envy their teacher. Does Perry still stay with Grandma? As usual there isn't any news to write about so I'll sign off for now.

"I'm tired of walking."

Write to

T.K.

••

Somewhere In Korea
2 July, 1951

Hi Folks [Wilson],

How is everyone. Me I'm getting harder to get along with every day. I guess it is the heat. One thing about it though we aren't allowed to lay around enough to get lazy and out of condition. I would sure hate to be on the line now. I guess this isn't as bad as the cold weather tho. I understand you've been working too hard again "Bee." I thought sure I had taught you better than that. I still believe anyone should take life easy as possible while they are young & enjoy it. I can't see waiting until you get old and grey headed. Well everyone to their own opinion I guess. You better slow down a little though, there's no sense in overdoing it when you don't have to. How do you like the cease fire rumors. Although I don't really believe it will come about perhaps it will be the start of a compromise that both sides can agree upon. Let's hope so. I know I'm satisfied to drop matters as they stand. Well I guess I had better close and prepare for a parade.

Write often
& don't work too hard,
T.K.

••

Somewhere In Korea
2 July, 1951

Dear Witts,

I'll try to drop you a line while no one is around to bother me. I am lying here in under shade tree close to a creek. We are still in Corps reserve so I've been getting a bit more rest. I don't have to worry about any one sneaking up on me at least. It is getting quite warm here now. I'd say about 100° through the day but the nights cool off quick so as usual I have a slight cold. I'm still listening to this cease fire talk but it looks like there won't be much more take place until they've had their meeting now. I doubt if the Chinese will accept Ridgeway's terms anyway. They've lost a lot of men and we've run them out of South Korea but there seems to be no end to their manpower. We have another parade this afternoon at six-thirty. We wear fatigues on these parades but we shine our helmets and don't look so bad. Is V.O.[1] still getting fat? I may want to borrow some of his weight when I get back although I feel like I'm gaining a little back myself. We have a new platoon leader now, a Second Lieutenant and honestly I believe I know more about this life over here than he does. I hope he gets transferred soon as this is no place to have to obey someone who doesn't know much. I guess I'll sign off now as there still isn't anything to write about.

> Hoping to
> See you soon,
> *T. K.*

....

12 July, 1951

Dear Mom,

Just a line to let you know I'm back with the company and well. I was pretty sick for a few days there but seem to feel all the better for it now. They had just sent my mail to the hospital when I got back so I still haven't heard from anyone. I'll probably get a letter tonight though. It seems like I manage to get about one a day at least when I'm here. How's the weather at home. It's certainly hot here, very sultry this afternoon. Excuse the writing but I'm lying on my back with my knees for a desk and am too hot and lazy to move. I've just washed a t-shirt and handkerchief out here in the creek, which seems to be about all I ever wash. Well guess I'll sign off so

"...a t-shirt and handkerchief... seems to be about all I ever wash."

> Write soon
> *T.K.*

---

1 V.O. is Virgil O. Witt.

Dear Mom, Dad, & All,

Just a line or two today to let you know I'm alright. We are back on the line, have been since the sixteenth, so are very busy. Our positions are dug in on a sandy slope of a steep hill and it is very difficult to get a bunker built that will stand up. One especially has caved in three times, once hurting my assistant BAR man's back so we're a man short. I'm going to try and get it rebuilt so it will stay today, so I'll have to make this brief.

"...on a sandy slope... it is very difficult to get a bunker built..."

There were four Chinese came in day before yesterday and surrendered. They claimed the Chinese Regiment in front of us all wanted to surrender so we've been hoping. We've set up a loud speaker system up here to tell them to come on in but so far haven't had any success. Anyhow *they* aren't giving us any trouble to speak of so don't worry about me.

I received a package of Vienna sausage and stuff from you yesterday but so far have not seen any candy. I got a picture from Joan yesterday. It's really good of her. Well guess I'll close for now and get back to work. I have not heard much news of this cease-fire talk recently sure hope they are still meeting. Write soon.

Love,
T.K.

July 21, 1951

Dear Folks [Wilson],

Just a line to say "hi." How are the Wilson's these days, me as good as ever I guess. I am back on the line close to Inje now. We came back up the sixteenth but I've been too busy to write. I know that sounds like a lame excuse but standing guard just about all night and building bunkers all day and trying to get a couple winks of sleep in between times I have been pretty busy. I have to go now as someone is calling me so will finish this later.

Well I'll try again as we just finished another bunker maybe I'll get to finish this, this time. It has been raining for nearly three days now and I've sure been miserable. When we have pretty nights, one man can pull guard and let the other one sleep but when it's raining and you can't hear or see very well either, I make everyone around me stay awake at night. How do you like your new home? You all move so much I guess it doesn't seem strange or new to you anymore. I've been wondering if you were going to stay in one place any length of time ever. I don't think we'll be on line so long this time as we have been in the past the first and second of the thirty-eighth are still in reserve so possibly one of them will relieve us before too many days. I understand the Ninth Regiment, which is also part of the 2nd Division, is working it that way. Their 3rd Battalion, which is on our left flank, is just going to stay for ten days then one of the other two will relieve them. If that happens to us we'll only have about five more days up here. I think I'll be up for rotation about the last of next month or possibly in September. If so I should be home sometime in October. If things stay pretty quiet over here I'm pretty sure of that. Well guess I'd better sign off so I can get this mailed.

"...I've sure been miserable...."

Write to,
Tony

. . . .

July 22, 1951

Dear Witts,

I'll try to write a line or two this afternoon, possibly I won't be disturbed before I finish it. I understand the Regimental Commander is coming around sometime this afternoon. He'll probably catch me sitting around and find something for me to do, he generally does. Well how are the Witts these days? Me, I'm alright, sweating out rotation and this cease-fire. I should get to leave here in September if this cease-fire doesn't beat that time. It's hard to tell now what might happen. I hope this cease-fire goes through first even though it might cause me to stay a bit longer. It's obvious we won't gain any more from this war anyway. The only thing I can see we've gained is that we've shown aggressor nations the U.N. will fight. I guess you've heard by now I'm back on the front lines but I am hoping we'll be relieved by the time you receive this. So far everything is pretty quiet. We've had a few men hurt themselves and a couple accidentally hurt. There have been several Chinese come in and surrendered. I understand and they all claim the Chinese Regiment in front of our vicinity want to surrender. It would be nice if they would without a shot fired. Well I'm going to close & try to get some sleep.

"It's obvious we won't gain any more from this war..."

Love,

T. K.

. . . .

SILVER STAR

Infantry-Artillery Team Takes Hill In 5-Day Fight [1]

SOMEWHERE IN KOREA – Self-propelled "long toms" set up in "artillery alley" on the central front were slamming shell after shell into Communist bunkers drilled deep into the rocks of the mountains. One by one, the Reds' fighting holes were being sealed shut.

The eyes of the artillery were infantrymen of the 38th "Rock of the Marne" Regiment. Living up to their name, they were in possession of hill 1179, "Gibraltar" of the central front. The towering mountain ridge had been hard won.

MEN OF THE 38TH fought five and a half days to pry the stubborn North Koreans from the rock fortress. With support from all of the 2d Division Artillery and direct fire from the heavy guns of the 72d Tank Battalion, the infantrymen had inched to the mountain crest. But in the final plunge it had

---

1 Tony enclosed this newspaper article in his August 14 letter with very little comment. The battle took place on July 30, 1951.

been rifle and bayonet and grenade that secured the Communist strong point.

THE REDS HAD planned well. Hill 1179 was a vantage point which gave them visual control of a vast curve of the Allies lines northeast of Yanggu. From it the enemy could call observed artillery fire along the UN main supply route, and could spot individual soldiers in their foxholes.

Artillery and air was not enough to drive the Communists from the hill. They had drilled their holes deep into the solid rock. They were nearly impregnable.

The attack on "Gibraltar" began with a three-day-and-night softening by Allied air and artillery. On the fourth morning the 38th kicked off in an attack that got them only 200 yards.

DIRECTLY IN FRONT of 1179 a weapon pocketed hill brought a company of Dutch soldiers to a standstill. Artillery fire seared the skies day and night to reduce that protecting bastion.

To the east of 1179 lay another ridge, also heavily manned with defending Communists. A company of the 23d Regiment, moving in for a diversionary attack, fought bitterly for a full day and then pulled back to let the artillery handle that one, too.

IT WAS THE ARTILLERY concentrations on these two outposts, coupled with a basic mistake in the Communists' defense, that finally permitted the 38th to take Hill 1179 with a minimum of casualties.

Once the two flanking hills were held down by artillery, the 2d Division Infantrymen were able to work around to the "blind spots" of the Red defenses. From that point it was a job of mountain climbing, and bitter work with the infantry's big stick – rifles, bayonets, and grenades. One by one the machine guns were silenced, Red defenders killed or routed.

THOSE WHO RAN were caught in the curtain of fire laid down by artillery behind 1179, designed to seal the hill from the rear to prevent the Communists from bringing up reinforcements.

Five days after they kicked off the attack "Rock of the Marne," men were occupying the holes the Communists had dug so carefully. From strategic points on the hill they were able to direct artillery fire on Communist positions that a few days before had been screened by the Korean "Gibraltar."

PROUDLY, MAJ. GEN. Clark L. Ruffner, 2d Division commander, passed on to his men the words of their corps commander: "Please express to the officers and men of the 38th Infantry Regiment and to those other Division elements which supported them in their gallant, determined and skilled seizure my sincere appreciation and admiration. The masterful reduction of this key terrain feature is in keeping with the brilliant record of your division."

And from General James A. Van Fleet, Eighth Army commander, the message: "I have carefully followed the operation of the Corps culminating in the capture of one high hill mass west of the 'Punch Bowl.' I wish to congratulate you and all the elements of your great corps and particularly the units of the 2d Division for a skillful and successful operation. It was particularly pleasing to me to observe the high morale and desire on the part of all hands to do the job."

This Silver Star citation (*opposite page*) describes Tony's role in this battle.

GENERAL ORDERS   11 October 1951
NUMBER   596

***   ***   ***

Section II

AWARD OF THE SILVER STAR—By direction of the President, under the provisions of the Act of Congress, approved 9 July 1918 (WD Bul 43, 1918), and pursuant to authority in AR 600-45, the Silver Star for gallantry in action is awarded to the following named enlisted men:

***   ***   ***

CORPORAL TONY K BURRIS, RA18313674, Infantry, United States Army, a member of Company L, 38th Infantry Regiment, 2d Infantry Division, distinguished himself by gallantry in action on 30 July 1951 in the vicinity of Taeusan, Korea. On that date during an attack on enemy positions, two platoons of Company L were pinned down by intense enemy small arms and automatic weapons fire from well built bunkers. Corporal Burris, with utter disregard for his own safety, crept forward to the enemy machine gun emplacement and threw several grenades into the bunker. At the sound of the grenade burst, Corporal Burris made his way forward into the enemy bunker and singlehandedly destroyed the remaining foe. Then standing on the top of the bunker, with enemy fire all about him, he called for the men in his platoon to advance. Corporal Burris' courageous actions so inspired the men that they overran the enemy positions. The gallantry in action demonstrated by Corporal Burris on this occasion reflects great credit upon himself and the military service. Entered the military service from Oklahoma.

***   ***   ***

BY COMMAND OF MAJOR GENERAL YOUNG:

OFFICIAL: RUPERT D GRAVES
                                   Colonel   GS
                                   Chief of Staff

DAVID B EMMONS
Lt Col   AGC
Adjutant General

....

THE STORM CONTINUES

....

U.N. on the offensive; Tony's ranking down and up

August 18: *U.N. forces including L Company begin an attack on what would become known as Bloody Ridge.*

Tony has little tiffs with his platoon officer and loses rank. He neither laments the demotion nor repents. Tony regains rank and more, but loses R&R because of higher rank. He becomes "acting second lieutenant" leading the platoon. He remains more concerned about rotation than rank while achieving the rank of Staff Sergeant.

Bloody Ridge after heavy fighting and deforestation, 1951.

Aug 4, 1951

Dear Folks [Burris],

Just a line before dark to let you know I'm ok. We are building positions on another hill now north of Inje, but unlike the last time we had to fight for these positions so I don't much think we'll be pushing after we leave this hill. I believe we will go back into reserve. I have been demoted & promoted several times in the past few weeks. My platoon officer, a new one, and I got into several little tiffs and he took my squad away from me and made me assistant squad leader & then reduced me to a rifleman. But things did not run so smooth for him so I am assistant platoon sargeant. We will probably get into trouble again and I'll lose that though so I guess I'm still too independent. Well it's getting dark so I will close for now. I received Bee's hot sauce but never have received your candy.

Love,

T.K.

··

Aug. 6, 1951

Dear Mom, Dad, & All,

Just a line today to say "hello." I still don't have much time for writing so it may be several days before I can write again. I have been promoted to platoon sargeant now so you can imagine just about how busy I am with my new duties and all. If I hadn't got the job as platoon sargeant I would have left yesterday for five days R.&R. in Japan but now will have to wait until I get back in reserve as platoon *sargeants* can't leave while on the line. It was sure a surprise to *hear* that I'm due for R.&R. I figured rotation would catch me first. As it is I'll be

"I have been promoted to platoon sargeant..."

rotated, I'm sure, shortly after I go to Japan. There are two men in the company that have more line time than I have & about six more with rear issue line time enough to be ahead of me on the rotation list. I guess I'll make my staff sargeant rating before I go back. The last time I was put in for it they wanted to see my actions as a squad leader a little more. I guess someone is satisfied as they gave me a bigger job. Well I saw chow come up just now so I'll go get everyone ready to eat.

Write often,

T.K.

∙∙

Aug. 9, 1951

Dear Wilsons,

Just a line to let you know & you can let all the folks know, I'm alright. We are still on the line but aren't having much trouble as yet. I think we'll be pulled back in reserve before very long. I'll write as soon as we do so you all can quit worrying. I'm acting platoon leader now and have been put in for staff again. The first time I was put in, they wouldn't make me because they said I didn't have enough experience as a squad leader. Squad leader calls for sargeant first class & platoon leader calls for the rank of second lieutenant. Acting Second Lieutenant Burris, how does that sound '*ha*'. If I can hold my job a couple more weeks I'm pretty sure I'll make staff & if I'm over here one month after that I'm pretty sure I'll make S.F.C. but I think I'll be rotated before then. I found out today one of my squad leaders is fifth on rotation list in the company. He was assigned to the Second Division on the 1st of December and has one month's bad time against him so that puts me I'll say somewhere between sixth and twelfth. In one month's time

> **"Acting Second Lieutenant Burris, how does that sound?"**

the way they're going now, if they keep it up, I should be leaving here. The way this goes over here though you can't be sure. To rotate on the new rotation plan one needs what they call twenty-four months constructive service. I figure I have thirty one. Of course I'll have to wait my turn but it shouldn't be long until it is my turn. They count one day front line time equal to four days constructive service so you can figure by the end of this month I'll have the equivalent of thirty-four months constructive service. I know for sure I'll get five days R&R to Japan as soon almost as we go into reserve if I don't get rotated by then so I'll get to relax a wee bit one way or another. I was scheduled to go on R&R the next day after I made platoon sargeant but while on the front lines platoon sargeants don't go on R&R. Two days later our platoon leader, Lieutenant Gould was transferred to another company so I took over. Our Company Commander doesn't seem to have much faith in me as yet. He has been with the company for about a month now and because I'm a corporal he seems to doubt whether I can handle it or not. I think I can satisfy him as long as we're on the line but when we go back into reserve I have my doubts. Let's hope I rotate quickly huh. Well guess I'll close for now as I'm about out of words so write soon & often.

    T.K.

P.S. I received your package of hot stuff several days ago. I & a Spanish boy, one of my squad leaders, finished it today. Sure enjoyed it. It gave these c-rations a little flavor.

Aug 14, 1951

Dear Mom, Dad, & Kids,

    Just a few lines today to let you know I'm still ok. We are still up on the line but expect to be pulled off very shortly. When we do go back in reserve I am confident I'll be rotated before coming back on the front line thus it will be a relief to get back into reserve. One of my squad leaders came to Korea in December & is the only one I know in this company that beat me in line time here in Korea. He is fifth on the rotation list so I should be leaving also before long. If I don't forget about it before I mail this I'm going to send an article to you from one of the papers we receive here. We are now dug in on hill 1179 & with the help of K. Company took this hill a week or so ago. Almost *two* weeks now I guess. There isn't really much to write about so I'll close for now saying,

"hoping to see you soon."

T.K.

• •

Aug. 22, 1951

Dear Folks [Burris],

I'll try to write a line or two today to let you know I'm ok. The weather has been wet and chilly for the last two weeks. I'm still waiting to go into reserve. We've been

"Excuse the writing as I'm in a dark bunker..."

on the line now since July 15th so it's about time we get a break. I made my staff sargeant a few days ago so I'm ready to leave now. It's beginning to look like no one is going to rotate until we get back in reserve but maybe I'll get my turn when we do. I got a letter from Wanda today and she seems to think I might be on my way home but worse luck I'm not. It will sure be nice to get off this hill[1] and get a chance to clean

---

1 The platoon endured miserable and depressing conditions while holding that strategic hill for weeks. Supply line limitations meant that they could not have the decaying bodies removed. Lieutenant Dudley C. Gould describes these problems in graphic detail in his books, *Follow Me Up Fool's Mountain* and *You Tremble Body*.

up a bit. I can't understand why you haven't been hearing from me as I've been writing pretty regular. I imagine you have received a letter by now though or at least someone should have. Excuse the writing as I'm in a dark bunker and can't see very well. I guess T.D. and Perry will be starting to school soon huh. How do you think they'll like it. I don't imagine the teachers will appreciate it. I guess I'll close for now so tell everyone "hello" &

Write Often

T.K.

....

··

FIGHTING VAGABONDS

··

U.N. forces attacking; Tony's friends Borbon, Saladanya, and Sanchez

September 13: *U.N. forces begin the attack on Heartbreak Ridge. A mistake they made turned into a success, so Company L earns the moniker "Fighting Vagabonds."*

Tony gets five days of R&R. He writes about "three Spanish boys" who were "the best all around soldiers I have known," but only Steve Sanchez remains alive at the time of Tony's letter. In fact, Steve and Tony are the only surviving members of the nine-man squad Tony led in May. The rotation "carrot" keeps moving.

Troops on Bloody Ridge, 1951

Dear Mom,

How are you these days? I am ok I reckon. I haven't had much chance to write the last few days it's been so wet and sloppy. I am still on line for some cause or other. This is the longest period at one stretch this company has been on line since arriving in Korea. Today makes forty-six days on line and the longest stretch before had been forty-one. So I am still hoping to be relieved soon. I understand as soon as we go back into reserve I am going to get five days R&R to Japan and I still have hopes of rotating before coming out of reserve so I have quite a bit to look forward to if we ever get off this hill. I guess the kids will be in school about the time this reaches you. I imagine you'll be lost for a while huh. Is B.B. still in St. Louis? I hope he got his job. This weather is sure a mess. It'll rain for about four days then we'll have a nice day. Today I'd say the temperature is about 80° now possibly before dark it will start raining and drop down around 50°. I sure wish all the days would be as pretty as this one. Well I'll sign off for now.

> **"I am still hoping to be relieved soon..."**

Write often

T.K.

Hi Folks [Burris],

I'm sorry I haven't written sooner but have been Japan the last five days and kept pretty busy while there. I know you've been worried so decided to drop a line before going to bed. We are still on line but the company commander felt sorry for me I guess and let me go. I have no idea now how long I'll be over here as I believe this new rotation plan is going to slow me down considerably. It is certainly disappointing after having my hopes up so long. Well I guess I can put up with this country a little longer but I sure hate to. I'm going to sign off now. I know this is a poor letter but I'm tired so I'll try & write again soon.

Tony

....

Dear Witts,

I'll surprise you and write for a change although I don't know what I'll write. Just ramble on I guess. I just got back from five days of R & R in Japan. I sure had a swell time after being here in Korea this long. Of course I didn't do much resting but it was a big relief to get away a few days. You say V. O. is going to change jobs, maybe I would like to change jobs about now but I guess I'll stick with this one awhile. I got a letter from Dickie today and he's planning on going home soon. I sure hope he isn't as disappointed as I have been. I'm afraid this new rotation plan is going to foul me up. I believe it will take at least another month and possibly more now before I leave because of it. I don't understand it too well yet but I believe I'll have to stay at least that much longer. I'll bet Pamela is a case now huh. I can just see her getting fatter and meaner. Well I'm running out of words so tell everyone hello for me and write soon.

Love,

T. K.

"...maybe I would like to change jobs about now..."

Hi Folks [Wilson],

I'll write a line or two tonight while on phone guard if no one disturbs me. How is every one getting along these days? I'm doing alright I guess. We aren't taking more ground at least although still on line. Did you hear about our latest push. My battalion took a large hill, 1243, that the ROK Marines were supposed to take. It was supposed to have taken them six days to take it and someone misinterpreted our orders and we took it within fifty-six hours after we pushed off. It was supposed to have cost over five hundred casualties taking this hill. We had about seventy all told so we didn't do bad at all. As a matter of fact that's all we hear for the last few days. My company was the one that actually made the mistake and everyone seems to think we did it on purpose.

They call us the fighting Vagabonds of the Second Division now. So I guess that name will stick. The thirty-eighth, Rock of the Marne, Regiment has made even more of a name for itself over here than it did the last war. I would as soon do without some of that glory though and let someone else revel in it.

Our regiment has seen more combat than any here in Korea since January. Of course I've missed a lot of it. While I was in Japan in March they had a very big battle and lost a lot of men. In the action last May when my company was almost wiped out by mortars I was in the rear with some prisoners. I caught them just after it was over. In this last action on Hill 1243 I was in Japan so you see I've missed a lot of the worst fighting. Of course I haven't missed all of it but some of these guys have seen every battle since Hoengsong. There aren't any left besides myself in the company that went through that. Well I'll sign off and give your eyes a break so write soon and tell everyone hello.

Tony

....

Dear Mom, Dad, & Kids,

Just a few lines tonight to let you know I'm well-fed and healthy. I am still on line but there are troops out ahead of us a short ways so at the present time am not dodging bullets now at least. I was down at the rear C.P.[2] yesterday and all night last night taking a short course in artillery. Very little of it will ever do me any good but I know pretty well how they operate at least. I know one thing I would willingly trade places with anyone down there and *in* a short while I could do about as good a job, I personally believe. Of course I might be a wee bit prejudiced. I managed to change clothes & got caught in a shower yesterday so I'm in pretty good spirits as of now. I *am* beginning to believe we're never going to get back in reserve. We've been on line now since July 15th and before this time the longest we had been on line was forty-one days. You can imagine how disappointed we've been by not getting reserve before this. This new rotation plan has sure messed my rotation up. I figure it will be at least the last of October now before I get out of here and possibly longer. That will make about ten months I've been over here so as you see this *six* months rotation plan does not work very well. Excuse the scribbling but I cannot see to write very good. I'll try to do better next time.

Well I'll sign off for now so keep writing to

Tony

---

2 Command Post

Hi Wilsons,

I'll try to write a line or two tonight before I go to bed. We aren't on the front lines anymore but still no reserve. We are now acting as a sort of second line just in case anything breaks through we stop it. I've about lost hope on getting reserve so I won't dwell on that. This new rotation plan is going to slow me down for a couple months at least. I've been in this same company for eight months now and it looks like it will take ten or eleven to get out of it. So it looks like this six months rotation business was just a pleasant dream. Don't expect me home until the latter part of November or December now and before then they may figure out a new method of rotation. You asked in your letter about my Spanish friend & if he received packages. It's rather a long story but I'll give you a little of his history. Back in March a week or so after I came back from the hospital three Spanish boys were assigned to the squad in which I was assistant squad leader. They were the best all around soldiers I've known since I've been in the army so I quickly made friends with them. Borbon was the one I liked best, the one who put his life in danger more than once for me. You've heard me speak of bunker hill I know. Anyway back in May Steve Sanchez[3] was wounded in that fifth phase offensive. He returned to the platoon on May 30th. On the push to Inje, about May 22nd Saldanya was killed. In the latter part of July Borbon, now a corporal, was wounded & returned from the hospital the day

"...three Spanish boys... were the best all around soldiers I've known..."

---

3 Steve Sanchez received a Silver Star for his role in the battle on May 15, 1951 near Inje.

I went on R&R, the second of September I believe. While I was in Japan Corporal Borbon was killed while our company was taking Hill 1243. Steve Sanchez now my assistant platoon sargeant is the only one left out of that squad of nine men I had in May. So you see you could hardly send a package to Corporal Borbon now. Anyway he had too much pride to accept it. By the way I'm in for sargeant-first-class again and the company commander told me tonight, as soon as it came through I was going in for master. That pretty well takes care of all the news so I'll sign off saying

> **"...Sanchez... is the only one left..."**

> Write To
>
> *Tony*

....

··

HEARTBREAK RIDGE

··

U.N. offensive continues; Tony's last letter

October 1: *U.N. forces continue to attack.*

Tony promoted to Sergeant First Class and then chewed out. Company L in reserve and standing for inspection, they will go back on line soon. Tony expects another promotion. He asks for stationery, handkerchiefs, and hot sauce. He has little faith in the new rotation plan.

Heartbreak Ridge in foreground, view northwest, Mundung-ni Valley far right.

Hi Folks [Burris],

I'll write a few lines *tonight* to let you know I'm alright. How is everyone there? We've been in reserve since the 22nd. I'm pretty sure it won't last long the twenty third are still on line. We had a big inspection today by Colonel Mildren, our Regimental commander so we've been running around in circles all day. A rumor is out we'll be moving over in the eastern sector when we go back on line. If so perhaps the hills won't be so tall at least. The land over there is supposed to be more rolling than it is over here. I don't know when I'll get to come home perhaps next month some time but not certain at all so I'm not going to plan too strongly on it. By the way I am now sargeant-first-class. The company commander told me about it and then chewed me out for not having the correct stripes on. Well that's about all the news so I guess I'll sign off.

Tony

Dear Wilsons,

How is everyone these days. I am doing alright I suppose. You probably know that I've made sargeant-first-class by now. I remember you saying in one of your letters that if I hadn't got sent to the hospital I might have made tech before I got out. Sargeant-first-class is the same as tech and I've been put in for master. Of course I might not make it. After all I've only been the army less than fourteen & one-half months. I realize that's going a little too fast but my job calls for second-lieutenant so of course that would be taken into consideration. We've been in reserve now for about twelve days but I'm sure we'll be going back on line before this letter reaches you. We only pulled back to train the new men to work with the outfit. Our battalion has built quite a name for itself recently. I'm sure you've been hearing lots about the thirty-eighth regiment. They've been assigning, as a rule, a certain objective to the first or second bat. The last four of their objectives they would be unable to take so they would call the third bat. and we'd take it for them. Our battalion commander has made a big name for himself that way. He is a good tactician alright but if he didn't have good cooperation from his men he wouldn't go anywhere. I've learned that a man is in more danger from the enemy if his back is turned to him, while retreating, than he is while charging him. Our whole battalion seems to think along those lines so that is one reason why we have so much success. Well enough of that. The nights are beginning to get pretty cool now but most of the days have been warm recently.

"I may get out of here somewhere around the first of December..."

I'm afraid I'm going to get another taste of cold weather before I get out of here. If the rotation plans aren't changed I may get out of here somewhere around the first of December. Of course one can't tell for sure as yet. Under the old plan they were getting the men out pretty quick through June but in August they practically stopped altogether. If they had kept the old plan operating about the same way I would have been home by now. If we are on line and the fighting is bad this Regiment almost stops rotation completely. You asked in your letter if I needed anything. I could use some stationery, a couple handkerchiefs, as I have a bad cold, and some more hot stuff. Those C-rations don't go down very good anymore without something to give a tang to them. Well it's getting late and I have to rise early so guess I'll close for now. I won't write mom as I wrote her a few days ago so let her know when you receive this. Also the Witt family. Tell everyone

Hello,

Tony

Tony was killed in action on October 9, 1951 in the battle for Heartbreak Ridge.

....

MEDAL OF HONOR

....

Master Sergeant Steve Sanchez[1] chose to honor Tony with a very personal letter that describes his friend and fellow soldier. He sent this letter to Tony's sister, Loretta Burris Wilson, predicting honors yet to come.

Dec 2, 1951
NORTH KOREA

Mrs Wilson:

Let me tell you a few things. First; in Tony you have lost a man that in my way of thinking was not only a great man, a brave man, but also a good man. Never has this company mourned the loss of one of its men as much as it did Tony's. Please, please do not think that I am trying to build Tony up

----

1 Steve was now the last survivor of the three Spanish boys that were Tony's closest friends in Korea, and he was the last survivor of the squad Tony led in May 1951. Steve received a Silver Star for his valor on May 15, 1951 near Inje, Korea.

Mrs Wilson:
　　　　Let me tell you a few things. First; in Tony you have lost a man that in my way of thinking was not only a great man, a brave man, but also a good man. Never has this company mourned the loss of one of its' men as much as it did Tony's. Please, please do not think that I am trying [...]

in any way. Not enough praise can be given to men like him. About Tony's death, the only thing I can tell is that he died right after taking an enemy bunker by himself. Before that he had lead attacks on two enemy hills, personally knocking out 3 enemy bunkers. When Tony was killed, he died instantly. I don't think he knew what hit him. A bullet caught him between his eyes. In the near future, Mrs. Wilson, you will probably know just how great a soldier Tony was. You may wonder about that statement now, but in the near future you will know.

Steve Sanchez
M/Sgt. – Infantry

CITATION

Nearly nine months after Tony's death, President Harry S. Truman signed the document authorizing the Medal of Honor for Sergeant First Class Tony K. Burris.

The President of the United States of America, authorized by Act of Congress March 3, 1863 has awarded in : name of The Congress, the Medal of Honor, posthumously, to

SERGEANT FIRST CLASS TONY K. BURRIS, USA

for conspicuous gallantry and intrepidity at the risk of his life above and beyond the call of duty in action with the enemy:

Sergeant Burris, Infantry, United States Army, a member of Company L, 38th Infantry Regiment, distinguished himself by conspicuous gallantry and outstanding courage above and beyond the call of duty in the vicinity of Mundung-ni, Korea, on 8 and 9 October 1951. On 8 October, when his company encountered intense fire from an entrenched hostile force, Sergeant Burris charged forward alone, throwing grenades into the position and destroying approximately fifteen of the enemy. On the following day, spearheading a renewed assault on enemy positions on the next ridge, he was wounded by machine gun fire but continued the assault, reaching the crest of the ridge ahead of his unit and sustaining a second wound. Calling for a 57mm recoilless rifle team, he deliberately exposed himself to draw hostile fire and reveal the enemy position. The enemy machine gun emplacement was destroyed. The company then moved forward and prepared to assault other positions on the ridge line. Sergeant Burris, refusing evacuation and submitting only to emergency treatment, joined the unit in its renewed attack but fire from hostile emplacements halted the advance. Sergeant Burris rose to his feet, charged forward and destroyed the first emplacement with its heavy machine gun and crew of six men. Moving out to the next emplacement, and throwing his last grenade which destroyed this position, he fell mortally wounded by enemy fire. Inspired by his consummate gallantry, his comrades renewed a spirited assault which overran enemy positions and secured Hill 605, a strategic position in the battle for "Heartbreak Ridge". Sergeant Burris' indomitable fighting spirit, outstanding heroism and gallant self-sacrifice reflect the highest glory upon himself, the Infantry and the United States Army.

Harry Truman

EPILOGUE

Buried With Military Honors

There is no way to soften the blow of having a son killed in action, but the continuous flood of communications to the family was extremely brutal.

- A telegram on October 31, 1951 from Major General Wm. E. Bergin, Adjutant General of the Army, to Mrs. Mable A. Burris, expressed deep regret that Tony K. Burris was killed in action in Korea on October 9.
- A copy of Final Report B 3113 dated 1 Nov 1951, was received by Tony's mother Mable confirming that Burris, Tony Kenneth was killed in action on 9 Oct 1951.
- A condolence letter from General Mathew Ridgeway was sent to Mrs. Burris on November 8.
- Colonels Mildren and Mullaney each sent a condolence letter on November 14.
- A letter on November 26 informed Mrs. Burris that a Purple Heart had been awarded posthumously to Tony.
- A letter dated January 8, 1952 from Colonel James B. Clearwater informed Mrs. Mable A. Burris that the remains of her son, the late Sergeant Tony K. Burris, "were recovered in Korea and evacuated to the mortuary in Kokura, Japan. Where they will be prepared by qualified morticians and casketed by carefully trained personnel as the first step in returning them to the United States."
- A telegram on January 19, 1952 informing Mrs. Mable A. Burris that the remains of Sergeant First Class Tony K. Burris "are en route to the United States" and asking the next of kin to immediately telegraph collect to the Quartermaster General "advising the town or city or national cemetery to which the remains are to be delivered." The telegram explained that if a private funeral director is involved, the government will reimburse "in an amount not

to exceed one hundred and twenty five dollars."

• A letter on January 25 from Colonel James B. Clearwater informed Mrs. Mable A. Burris "the body will, upon arrival in the United States, be reshipped to the Matheny Funeral Home of Blanchard, Oklahoma."

• A telegram on February 7 to Mrs. Mable A. Burris advised that the remains of SFC Burris would depart Oakland on February 8, escorted by SFC John C. May, to arrive in Norman at 1:20 a.m. on February 11 and requests that the "funeral director receive remains and escort at Norman."

Nearly four months after Tony's death, on February 11, 1952, the funeral was held in the First Baptist Church. The following military graveside service at the Blanchard Cemetery ended with a twenty-one gun salute and the playing of *Taps*. SFC John C. May left after the burial.

The Burial, February 11, 1952

The Legacy

Tony K. Burris was deprived of his life at the age of 22 while fighting for his country in a war that he did not understand. He killed enemy that he did not hate, dislike, or denigrate; and he became a highly decorated hero of the "The Forgotten War." His fellow soldiers, veterans, Blanchard, the Choctaw Nation, the State of Oklahoma, the U.S. military and government, South Korea, and many others continue to honor Tony K. Burris for his courage and sacrifice.

Silver Star: On Memorial Day, May 30, 1952, at Fort Sill Oklahoma, Mable Burris received the medal on what would have been Tony's twenty-third birthday.

Congressional Medal of Honor: Sid and Mable travelled by train to Washington, D.C. arriving on August 13, 1952. They received an escorted tour of D.C. that afternoon. On August 14, General Omar Bradley of the U.S. Army presented the Congressional Medal of Honor and they flew home.

Sid and Mable Burris in Washington, D.C.

Junior Class of '52 Plaque: In 1952, the Junior class of the Blanchard High School presented the school a plaque honoring Tony.

Fort Lewis, Washington: L Company, 3rd Battalion, 38th Infantry Regiment of the Second Infantry Division named their day room the Tony K. Burris Memorial Day Room to honor one of their own in 1955. In 1957, they also named the Tony K. Burris Field in his honor.

Army Reserve Center Chickasha, Oklahoma: On September 25, 1960, Senator Robert S. Kerr gave the dedication speech for the Tony K. Burris United States Army Reserve Center.

Mable Burris cuts the ribbon at the Army Reserve Center dedication ceremony.

Seoul, Korea: In April 1962, Building 2552 at the Yongsan Military Reservation in Seoul was dedicated as Burris Hall with a bronze plaque commemorating Tony's "heroic deeds in combat" displayed in a "prominent location of honor."

Burris Hall, Seoul, Korea (circa 1962)

NCOA of Oklahoma City, Oklahoma: In 1967, the newly formed Oklahoma City chapter of the Noncommissioned Officers Association became the SFC Tony K. Burris Chapter.

Medal of Honor Grove, Valley Forge, Pennsylvania: As part of the USA Bicentennial Celebration, Freedoms Foundation planted a tree honoring Tony K. Burris in the Medal of Honor Grove on July 4, 1976.

VFW Post, Blanchard, Oklahoma: In May 1981, the Blanchard VFW Post officially became the Tony K. Burris Post #3608. The Post annually awards the "Tony K. Burris Post #3608 Achievement Award" to a Junior High School Student and to a Senior High School Student.

1981: Mable Burris with the first Achievement Award recipients

Recipients of the Tony K. Burris VFW Post 43608 Achievement Award was presented to Brent Mitchell for High School and Dawn Reldwell for Junior High. They are pictured here with Mrs. Mabel Burris, mother of Tony K. Burris for whom the award was named. This is the first time for the award to be presented.

Blanchard Public Schools: On November 7, 2007, the Education Foundation inducted Tony K. Burris into the Blanchard Hall of Fame.

The Oklahoma Military Hall of Fame: On November 9, 2013, Tony K. Burris was inducted into the Oklahoma Military Hall of Fame.

Choctaw Legacy Film, *Tony K. Burris*: In 2013, the Choctaw Nation commissioned the making of a legacy film honoring the Choctaw Korean War hero Tony K. Burris.

On May 29, 2017, **U.S. Highway 62** in Blanchard was designated as The SFC Tony K. Burris Memorial Highway. The honors and tributes continue. Tony has not been forgotten.

Statue of
Tony K. Burris
in downtown
Blanchard, Oklahoma.

Memorial, Blanchard, Oklahoma: On September 15, 2007, the Tony K. Burris Memorial was dedicated and his statue unveiled on the northeast corner of Main Street and U.S. Highway 62 in downtown Blanchard. The statue, paid for by the Choctaw Nation, stands on land donated by the Pioneer Telephone Company. Tony's hand points in the general direction of the pool hall he frequented.

The Documenters

Family: Loretta Burris Wilson made sure that the memory of Tony stayed alive. During Tony's military service, she shared his letters in newspaper articles. Later she shared the notifications of coming awards and ceremonies, as well as giving personal interviews for newspaper articles. She provided Betty Lewis with letters and telegrams to be included in Betty's classes and memorial book. She did the same for Thomas Hedglen to use in his publication about Tony. She and her sister Wanda Burris Witt visited Burris Field at Fort Lewis, Washington and she was at the 1976 ceremony in Valley Forge, Pennsylvania. She also wrote letters to the Korean government leading to the naming of Burris Hall in Seoul, South Korea.

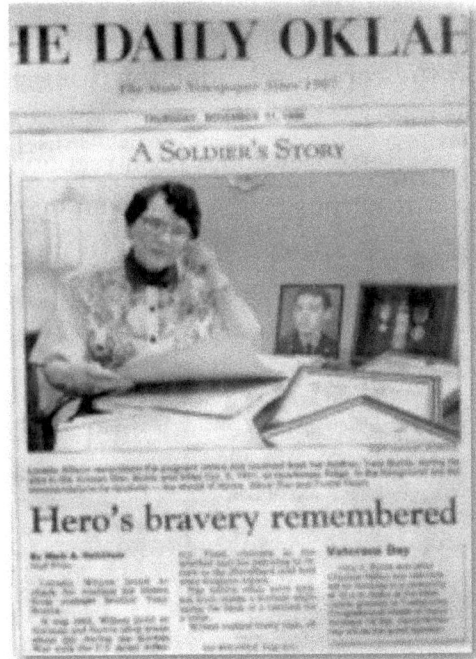

Loretta and her sister **Jennifer Burris Kniss** prepared and gave presentations honoring Tony for decades on various occasions. More recently, Loretta, Wanda, Karen, Jen, and Judy provided information and interviews to the makers of the Choctaw Legacy Film, and they are featured in that film. Also recently, Jen initiated contact with the Oklahoma Military Hall of Fame, leading to Tony's induction in 2013. Jen and her sister Karen Burris McConnell have become the primary points of contact for information about Tony.

Betty Binyon Lewis: Betty Lewis was a Blanchard teacher from 1958 through 1995. She prepared and taught class sessions to all her students on courage and honor. She used Tony's story and field trips to his grave to motivate Blanchard students for those classes. Tony's twin brothers, Terry and Perry, and twin sisters, Judy and Jen, remember those particular classes quite well. Betty also wrote *A Memorial to Tony Kenneth Burris*, a book available in the Blanchard Library. We have used materials from her book when original copies were no longer available, and we have benefitted from viewing a video of her presentation at the ceremony inducting Tony into the Blanchard Hall of Fame.

Betty Lewis has been recognized for her many contributions to the school and community, including the

Seventh graders learned a little history at the Blanchard Cemetery last week English Teacher, Betty Lewis point out Tony Burris' grave to Mike Grady, Timmy Outon, Sean Bell, Brian Jervis, Clinton Roberts, Brad Clagg, Rhonda Goucher, Toby James, Laura Spurgin and Angela Holt.

Betty Lewis's class visits Tony's grave (date unknown).

naming of the Betty Binyon Lewis Alumni Center in her honor. She graduated from Blanchard High School in 1951, the year Tony died.

Thomas Hedglen: Thomas wrote *The Tony Burris Story in Two Parts*. The first part blends materials and letters provided by Loretta Wilson, Betty Lewis, and military documents, to provide a strategic military context to Tony's service. The second part describes the planning, coordination, and funding of the statue, as well as documenting the September 7, 2007 ceremony for the Tony K. Burris Memorial. This publication was prepared for, and presented to, the 10th Annual Conference of the Center for the Study of the Korean War in February 2009; a copy is available at the Blanchard Library.

The Family 1952-2017

Tony made it clear that he felt there is no place like home, and his family evidently continues to agree. His brothers and sisters lived most of their lives near Blanchard, and those whose employment took them away all returned to the home county. Here is a thumbnail sketch of the next sixty-plus years of the family members mentioned in Tony's letters.

2016: Burris family. Back Row (L-R): T.D., Karen, Jen, Larry Wilson, Perry, Judy, Jimmy McConnell. Front Row: Burnett, Pam Witt

Sid and Mable: Tony's mother became a dietary cook at the Oklahoma Mental Institution in Norman, and Sid quit farming to work at Tinker Field Air Force Base in Oklahoma City. In 1957, Sid took a disability retirement. In retirement, Sid bought/sold/traded cars, won at poker, and briefly owned and operated beer joints. In 1961, they left the farm and purchased a house in Blanchard less than a mile from where Tony's statue now stands. Mable retired circa 1971. Sid died in 1973. Mable was pleased to purchase a new brick home in SW Oklahoma City in 1979, where she lived until she passed away in 1991.

Loretta and Doyce: Loretta and Doyce Wilson raised two children, Larry Wayne (1942) and Teresa Ann (1955). Doyce fought in Europe throughout World War II. He graduated from Oklahoma University with a BS in Engineering in1954. Before his retirement in 1980,

he worked for Mobil Oil Company in Oklahoma, Texas, Georgia, and Pennsylvania. Loretta worked for years as a bookkeeper and for many more as a mother, homemaker, and Sister Bea. In 1980, they returned to live in SW

Oklahoma City, twenty miles from Blanchard. Doyce passed away in 2006 and Loretta in 2015.

Wanda and Virgil: Wanda and Virgil Witt lived and raised their daughter Pamela Janet (1947) in SW Oklahoma City. Wanda worked at Tinker field and the IRS before retiring. Virgil fought in the Pacific as a Marine during World War II. He drove for and retired from Roadway Sooner & Voss Truck Lines. After retiring, he owned and operated a lawnmower repair service. They lived in SW Oklahoma City until Virgil passed away in 2008 and Wanda in 2016.

Burnett and Bonnie: Burnett Burris married Bonnie Mae Gandy. They raised five children near Blanchard: Sidney Janet (1953), Teddy Ray (1954), Karen Michelle (Shelly) (1956), Carolyn Marie (1958), and Linda Sue (1959). Burnett worked for the FAA at the Will Rogers Airport before taking a

disability retirement. Bonnie worked for and retired from Western Electric in Oklahoma City. They continued to buy/renovate/sell real estate after retiring. Burnett passed away in 2017. Bonnie continues to live in Seminole, Oklahoma, about sixty miles from Blanchard.

Joan and Tubby: Joan married Myron C. (Tubby) Thomson, Jr. Tubby served in the Navy before working forty years as a Railroad Engineer for the Santa Fe Railroad. Joan worked as a loan processor in the mortgage banking industry. They raised two children, Carla Dianne (1956) and Scott David (1962) while living in SW Oklahoma City, Arkansas City, Kansas, and then on a farm near Tuttle, about ten miles from where Joan grew up. After retiring, they continued to farm. Tubby passed away in 2002 and Joan in 2014.

Karen and Jimmy: Karen married Jimmy Dwight McConnell. They raised three children: Marsha Gayle (1956), Toni Lynn (1958), and Tracy Denise (1965) in SW Oklahoma City before moving to a semi-rural neighborhood near Bridge Creek, about six miles from where Karen grew up. Karen worked at Western Electric. Jimmy owned and operated the J & L Auto Parts and Repair shop before retiring. Now in retirement, Jimmy has only two jobs: delivering auto parts and raising cattle.

Perry: Perry Burris married Linda Bonham. They divorced and he married Mary Jane Mernan. Perry and Mary had three children, Royce Lee (1970), Travis Ray (1973), and Troy Grant (1973). They divorced and he married Renate White, and they later divorced. Perry served in the Army. He worked as a painter before owning and operating a business specializing in painting equipment for oil field work and road building. Now retired, he continues to live on a farm within a mile of where he grew up.

T.D. and Diana: Terry Burris married Delores Ann (Pug) Allen. They had two children: Terry Doyce, Jr (1966) and Trina Dee (1968). They divorced, and T.D. married Diana Lynn Fredricks. T.D. worked as a foreman for Perry before he and Diana branched out to own and operate an upholstering service for road building equipment. T.D. is now retired, and Diana works for the

Chickasaw Nation. They live in Norman, Oklahoma, about twenty miles from Blanchard.

Jen and Don: Jen married Harry Dwaine Jones. They had one child, Jeffrey Dwaine (1969). They divorced, and Jen married Donald Hubert Kniss. Don, an Oklahoma

National Stockyard Commissioner, bought and sold cattle. Jen worked for General Electric and then worked at the Commissioner office with Don. Don passed away in 2013. Jen continues to live in SW Oklahoma City, about twenty miles from Blanchard.

Judy and Charlie: Judy married Donald Roy Moore. They had one daughter, Kellie Diana (1965). They divorced, and Judy married Gary Eugene Farmer. They divorced, and Judy married Charlie Simms. Charlie owns a lawn maintenance service. Judy worked for Western Electric and now runs a house cleaning service. They live close to Karen, about six miles from where Judy grew up.

Pam: Pamela Witt Stewart, now divorced, lives in Arlington, Texas. Pam has worked for Civil Service in the US Marshal Office in Dallas, TX and for a County Criminal Court Judge. She currently has a position with the Dallas Cowboys.

Larry and Twila: Larry married Twila June Hudson. They raised Lee Anne (1962) and Glen Allan (1963) in Virginia Beach, Virginia. Twila worked for and retired from EDO Corporation as a Senior Software Engineer. Larry retired as an Associate Professor of Computer Science at Old Dominion University. They live in Norfolk, Virginia.

Downtown Blanchard looks much the same as it did in 1950.

Blanchard Downtown Parade – circa 2010

Choctaw Heritage

Tony's parents were both Choctaw. Two of his grandparents, three of his great-grandparents, and four of his second great-grandparents were Choctaw. Samuel Sidney (Sid) Burris Jr. was born on March 6, 1906. He married Mable Agnes Curry, also a Choctaw, born April 6. Neither received a Choctaw land allotment.[34] They raised ten children, including Tony, while living on farms belonging to relatives.

Curry-Bench-James: Mable was one of five children born to Burnett and Clara Bench Curry (1886-1970). Clara was Choctaw; she and Mable's two older siblings each received Choctaw land allotments. Clara's parents, Nancy James Bench (1850-1894) and Henry Christopher (Chris) Bench Jr. (1849-1895), were both Choctaw. Nancy's parents, Benjamin James (1815-1896) and Mary Ann James (1822-1896), were both Choctaw. Chris's parents, Christopher Bench Sr. (1811-1855) and Catherine Crowder (1821-1868), were both Choctaw.

Nancy James Bench

---

34 The Choctaw Nation held their land in common until forced by the U.S. government to divide the land amongst tribal members. To receive land you had to be an Oklahoma Choctaw by blood or marriage by March 4, 1906. Sid was born two days too late and Mable was born just one month later.

Burris: Sid Burris was one of ten children born to Samuel Sidney Burris Sr., a Choctaw, and Florence Hayes Burris. Samuel Sr. received a Choctaw land allotment, as did Florence, and their three oldest children. Samuel Sidney Senior's parents were Gabriel Burris (1880-1928) and his second wife Polly Arnold Burris (1862-1950). Gabriel was the son of A. Samuel Burris (1796-1830) and Mary Meyers Burris, who were both Choctaw. After A. Samuel died, Mary Meyers and her children survived the Trail of Tears from Mississippi to Oklahoma where Gabriel became a respected Choctaw leader.[35]

Gabriel Burris

---

35 Page 90 in the *Leaders and Leading Men of Indian Territory: Choctaws and Chickasaws* by H. F. O'Beirne contains a short summary of the life of Gabriel Burris and this picture.

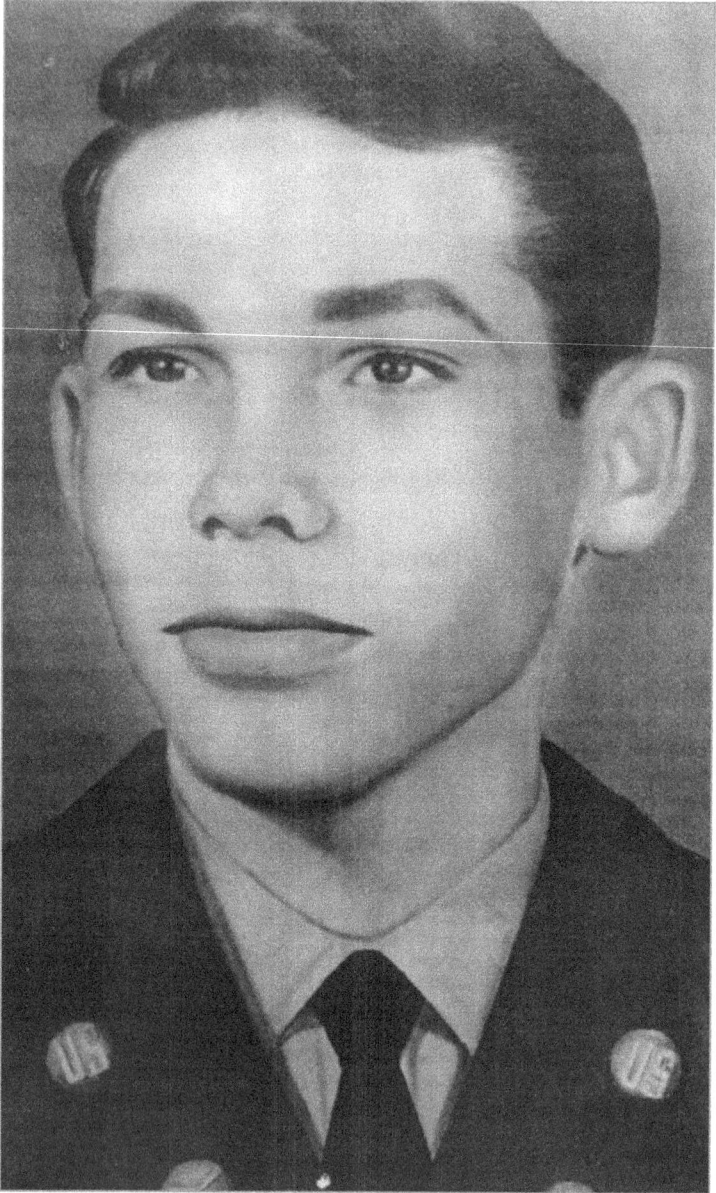

APPENDICES

Appendix A: League of Warriors

Soldiers know their own. This appendix will share the deep respect that fellow soldiers – Bill Maddox, James B. Luther, Bernie King, and Dudley C. Gould, Ronald Rosser and Linard White – held for Tony.

··

William S. (Bill) Maddox

Bill Maddox served in Korea with Tony from Hongsong to Heartbreak Ridge. In an undated document, he talks about sharing a pup-tent with Tony prior to the Hoengsong Massacre, and in a letter to Michael Davino describes their R&R together and plans for their future. Additionally, he has written a poem, "Memoriam – Tony K. Burris."

Rememering a Very Special Friend

It was February of 1951 and the weather was still bitterly cold. I was one of many replacements being sent to Korea. I had been assigned to Medical Company, 38th Infantry Regiment, U. S. Second Infantry Division and almost immediately placed with L Company, which had no Medics at that time. I shared a pup-tent with Tony K. Burris, who had been in Korea before I got there, however, like many replacements – neither of us had adequate winter clothing nor sleeping bags. Because of the extreme cold, we were miserable men!

Tony K. Burris had accepted the living conditions, but I complained continually. Tony improved our sleeping conditions better by putting down rice straw on the frozen ground, and how, I don't know, but had scrounged a couple of extra blankets. Tony was a quiet man, listening without comment to the men who had been there for several months. He asked questions only when needing additional information to assess what he had heard about the fighting and information about the enemy.

I never asked him, but I had the feeling that his ethnic background was Native American. Being together for several weeks gave each of us the opportunity to know each other better – and during that period of time, Tony managed to beg, borrow or steal some extra C-rations and cans of juice. He always shared what he managed to pick up by his bartering and scrounging. A more generous person you'd never find! He also had a great sense of humor, always making those around him feel better about their assignment in Korea. Finally, enough replacements arrived to fill up the platoons and I moved to a tent with one of the new Medic replacements, however, the friendship between Tony Burris and myself continued.

I was with Company L for almost nine months. During that time I watched Tony gain the respect of the platoon leaders, platoon sergeants, and the men in his platoon. He was what most of us would call a "good soldier" – always carrying out orders to the best of his ability. Tony and I had some rough times with Company L, the May Massacre, hills 1179 and 1243 and many, many combat patrols. We always found time for a few words, and as always, Tony would look at the positive side of our combat experiences. He advanced in rank, assumed more responsibility and was now considered one of the "old pros" of the company.

In September I was reassigned to the 3rd Battalion Aid Station. I missed the friends in Company L and continued *to go back and have as much contact with the enlisted men and officers as I could. On a couple of occasions I set up a forward Aid Station close to Company L during some combat operations. I saw many of the old-timers rotate home, and even though I was proud to see them go, I knew that their experience and expertise would be sadly missed by the Company. ...*

This quiet, likeable youngster from Oklahoma, who paid the ultimate price for his heroic action, received posthumously, The Congressional Medal of Honor, for his outstanding heroism and self-sacrifice.

Each year, since 1951, on October 9th, I remember Tony K. Burris and our friendship.

I remember our talks about all the things you talk about when you're young. I will never forget this man's friendship, his loyalty to friends and country, and his determination to always do his best in anything he undertook. Rest in peace my friend – I will never forget you and our friendship in some very trying times.

William S. "Bill" Maddox
Med/Co L, 38th Infantry Regt.
U. S. Second Infantry Division

Maddox Letter to Major Davino

Tuesday, May 3, 1994

Major Michael F. Davino,
HHC 4-325 AIR, ATTN: S3
Unit # 31530
AFO AE 09833

Dear Major Davino:
   Congratulations on your promotion! Sounds like you
have a very interesting ...
   My very best wishes for a safe and interesting assignment
in the Sinai, and again thanks for sending me photos of
the field and memorial to Tony K. Burris. Tony was a most
unusual young man, much higher caliber than many of the
GIs that I served with. I am sure he was either the offspring
of one Cherokee parent and one Caucasian, or possibly the
offspring of two Cherokee parents. Our first winter in Korea,
had it not been for Tony, I would have frozen my butt off. He
not only scrounged, but managed to get us through the coldest
part without one single winter garment, with the exception of
long-johns. At 19 years old – we both had planned hunting,
fishing, and most of all tomcatting – where we planned to
make as many Oklahoma and Arkansas girls happy as we
could. If he had been as big a hit in Arkansas as he was in
Japan – we would have had a ball. He was dark skinned,
with jet-black hair and eyes, and was one handsome dude.
Japanese girls followed him around – and I was proud to be a
buddy of his during our two trips to Japan together.
   Again, my best to you – and if and when you have a
little time, am always glad to get a letter from not only a
dedicated Army man – but from one that we need to have a
lot more of in today's Army.
   Sincerely,
   William S. (Bill) Maddox

Memoriam – Tony K. Burris

If you ever met him, you could never forget him,
and if you got to know him, he changed your life.

Tall and lanky like the woods he loved; yet easy-going
and calm like the lakes and rivers he found joy in.

This man was completely and ultimately consumed in the
simple offerings of this world.

Love of the woods, its lakes and streams, frosty mornings,
Oklahoma Hill Country and the men who served with
*   him formed*
the foundation this man lived for – and drew strength from.

Did he die in Korea? Are the lakes and rivers gone? Are the
friends and Hill Country gone? Certainly not – nothing is
truly gone until it is forgotten.

If you ever met him, you saw the woods, the lakes
*   and streams, the*
Oklahoma Hill Country and the loyalty to friends in his eyes.

And if you got to know him, you could feel his love of friends
and the military in his handshake.

Like all of nature's miracles – they and Tony K. will
*   never be forgotten.*
The next time you look out through the forests, gaze
*   across our lakes,*
or drive through forested hill country – look closely and you
*   will see him.*
The next time you watch a military parade or watch Old
*   Glory flying in the breeze, look closely and he will be there.*
He will always be.

Dedicated to my friend and comrade-in-arms Tony K. Burris, who was posthumously awarded The Congressional Medal of Honor for his self-sacrifice on October 9, 1951. Rest in Peace, Tony.

William S. (Bill) Maddox
Med/L Company, 38th Infantry
Second Infantry Division

James B. Luther

James Luther was Tony's platoon sergeant in the spring of 1951.

28 July 1952

Dear Mr. and Mrs. Burris,

It is with deep sympathy and fond remembrance that I write to you, the parents of one of the finest and outstanding soldiers I have had the pleasure to serve with, to pass on my condolences and heartfelt grievance for your bereavement.

Maybe I had better tell you just who I am and how I know Tony. I was in Co. L, 38th Inf as a Platoon Sergeant of 3d Plat. of which Tony was a member. When I first joined the Co. he was still a Private but recognizing good potential I made him a Squad Leader and a short while later he made Corporal. Then our company lost our 1st Sgt so there was a vacancy for that position. I was the one chosen so I left the 3d Plat. A short period elapsed and Tony still demonstrated top NCO potential so eventually he was made a Platoon Sergeant and advanced to the grade of Sergeant First Class. Then in August of 1951 I was given a Battle Field promotion to 2d Lt and left Co. L and went to our neighbor Co. K. But the friends I had in Co. L could never be forgotten. As is the case of friends made in combat are ones that will always be true and faithful. Then the big battle we had at Mundung-ni, Korea in October 1951 was one I shall never forget as it was this month I lost a friend, and you lost a son. Sometimes I just don't realize why our Lord above does such cruel things as take a man's life. Seems as if the ones he takes are always the best ones. Maybe He has a bigger job for him in the hereafter.

Maybe I had better close for now as I have undoubtedly

said too much already. I was just reading the issue of the Army Times newspaper dated 26 July 1952 and saw the article on Tony receiving the Medal of Honor. I knew he was put in for it but didn't know until today that he had received it.

I would like to say again that my heart is with you in your bereavement.

Sincerely yours,
James B. Luther,
2d Lt, Inf

....

Bernie R. King

Bernie King was with Tony on Heartbreak Ridge on October 8, 1951. He sent this letter five years later.

Layetteville, West Virginia
March 2, 1957

Dear Mrs. Burris,

I was very glad to receive your letter the other day and was glad you saw my letter in the True War Magazine. *I have been trying to locate Tony's family ever since the Korean War, but didn't know how to go about it until I saw the* True War Magazine *a few months ago, so I wrote them that I was a very personal friend of Tony's for about seven months of the war, which is the time we were together.*

Tony told me about Oklahoma and some of his family, but I had forgotten the name of the town he in which he lived. I always wanted to locate his family, and I finally did hear from you after all these years.

I also knew the Spanish boy, Steve Sanchez, very well. Tony, Sanchez and I were together all the time. I was with Tony up until October 8, which was the day I was wounded and also the day before he was killed, as you already know. The other boys of the Company came to the hospital a few days later and told me of his death. I learned the details from them. The boys also told me that he was put in for the C. M. H., and I learned later that his award had been approved, after I saw it in the Army Times *when I came back to the States a few months later. He was one of the bravest men I ever saw in combat. If anyone ever deserved this award, which is the Nation's highest, your son certainly did, but I*

know medals will never take the place of your great loss. I
offer my sympathy at this time, even it is a late time to do so.

I hope someday to make your acquaintance in person if
the opportunity ever comes along that I am in Oklahoma,
which I may be sometime. I would like to hear from you
again even if I never get a chance to see you in person.

I live in West Virginia now and work here. I live in a
small town, and I always pictured Tony's home town to be
something like this town, although I may be wrong.

I have four sisters. They are all married and have
families. I am still single.

Please write and tell me all about your son and family.
I would like to hear anything you write about Tony's honors
and his family.

A friend,
Bernie R. King

Dudley C. Gould

Dudley and Tony each received a Silver Star for Action in the same battle on July 30, 1951 near Taeuson, Korea. Lieutenant Gould led Tony's platoon from the end of April through the middle of August, and then led L Company before being transferred in early September. In the August 9 letter, Tony mentions that Lt. Gould left the platoon and that he, "Acting Second Lieutenant Burris," is now the platoon leader.

In "You Tremble Body"[1] on page 355, Dudley honors Tony and describes how and why he died.

I was surprised to learn that the old juggernaut companies, Item, Love[2] and King, were in harness again at Mundung-ni, Love leading with that professional Captain of the Regular Army. Much later, after I got back to the States, former medic, Bill Maddox of North Little Rock, Arkansas, told me that our Sergeant Tony Burris won a Congressional Medal of Honor at Mundung-ni the hard way. Grapevine told me the very day when Tony was among those who got it but the citation wasn't written while I was still in Korea. Colonel Duncan authored it and it was endorsed up the line to the Armed Forces Committee of Congress—

---

1 Dudley C. Gould wrote two books, *Follow Me up Fools Mountain: Korea 1951* (Southfarm Press) and *You Tremble Body* (Turner Publishing Company). The books feature his role and experiences leading the Third Platoon of L Company from April into May, 1951. Each book mentions Tony multiple times in positive ways.

2 L company aka Love company.

Rank and organization: *Sergeant First Class [promoted after he died], US Army, Company L, 38th Infantry Regiment, second Infantry Division. Place and date[3]: Mundung-ni, Korea, 9 November 1951. Entered service at: Blanchard, Oklahoma. G.O. No. 84, 5 December 1951.*

Citation:

SFC Tony K Burris, a member of Company L, distinguished himself by conspicuous gallantry and outstanding courage above and beyond the call to duty. On 9 November when his company encountered intense fire from an entrenched hostile force, SFC Burris charged forward alone, throwing grenades into the position and destroying approximately fifteen of the enemy. Spearheading a renewed assault on enemy positions, he was wounded by machine-gun fire but continued the assault, reaching the crest of the ridge ahead of his unit and sustaining a second wound. Calling for a 57mm recoilless rifle team, he deliberately exposed himself to draw hostile fire and reveal the enemy position. The enemy machine-gun emplacement was destroyed. The company then moved forward and prepared to assault other positions on the ridgeline. SFC Burris, refusing evacuation and submitting only to emergency treatment, joined the unit in its renewed attack but fire from hostile emplacement halted the advance. SFC Burris rose to his feet, charged forward and destroyed the first emplacement with its heavy machine-gun and crew of six men. Moving out to the next emplacement, and throwing his last grenade which destroyed this position, he fell mortally wounded by enemy fire. Inspired by his consummate gallantry, his comrades renewed a spirited assault which overran enemy positions and secured

---

3 Errata: The date of the action should be October 9, 1951, Tony entered the service in July not December, and he was Choctaw, not Cherokee.

a strategic position in the battle. SFC Burris' indomitable fighting spirit, outstanding heroism, and gallant self-sacrifice reflect the highest glory upon himself, the infantry and the US Army.

That was Tony Burris for you. I heard that Doc Carlson patched up Tony's thigh, shot him with morphine and began to write his tag when they heard a particularly nagging gook machine gun let loose. It was like a command to Tony; he brushed Doc aside saying it was only a nick and went limping half upright in a crazy one-man banzai, pulling the ring of a grenade. Then someone in the platoon up above yelled: "Medic! Medic!" Not long after that a voice yelled: "Never mind."

Burris told his assistant squad leader, Avery Olsen, on the eve of that singular ferocity, that, like J C, he had just about had it. He enumerated his weariness: Hoengsong, Twin Tunnels, Operation Killer, Massacre Valley, May Massacre. Task Force Joke, Inje and lately Hills 1100, 1179, 1181 and greatest catastrophe of all Magpie Mountain, 1243, where he lost the last of his old buddies, and he was good and tired of it day after day, losing buddies, being scared. He was sick of battles and constant mourning for dead guys he knew when they were happy and kidded around, and being half starved with death strewn all around him. And Tony, half Cherokee no man's boss every man's buddy, was a fierce Okie to his last battle, a goddamned heathen berserker (Scandinavian berserker: ber, bear; serke, shirt – wearing bearskin only, disdaining armor), a fierce individual, friend to all brother Indianheaders, fiend to enemies; to his mom and dad when he left to join the Army, a polite, modest gangly eighteen-year-old Southern Baptist boy.

"Now you be careful, Tony, and write and God will look after you and we will all pray."

The day before under sporadic sniping we finished clearing several approaches for our tanks to lay preparatory fire on the high hill trail on which Tony died.

. . . .

Ronald Rosser

Ronald Rosser, a Corporal at the time, received the Medal of Honor for his actions on January 12, 1952 while acting as a forward observer with company L's lead platoon. His citation is similar to Tony's in that he went up the hill alone three times to destroy enemy bunkers.

Rosser[4] was a forward observer on a nearby ridge on October 9, 1951. He saw Tony push the medics away and charge up the hill at an enemy bunker. He observed an enemy soldier raise a rifle to shoot the fatal bullet. Ronald knew of Tony by his reputation, though they were not in the same company nor close friends. He says that everyone liked and respected Tony as a soldier but he added that Tony could be "a bit of a clown" when not in battle. When asked why he and Tony repeatedly charged entrenched enemy positions alone, he replied that they did it to protect their men who were pinned down by enemy fire.

---

4 Retired Master Sergeant Rosser described Tony's death during a telephone interview, January 2013.

Linard White

After enlisting with Tony, Linard was sent to Alaska. This is the first of nine letters he would write to the Burris family.

Nov 8, 1951
Anchorage, Alaska

Dear Loretta,
Will answer your letter I received today, was kinda surprized to hear from you altho I was expecting a letter from some of the family. My mother sent me a newspaper clipping about Tony. It just didn't seem possible that it could happen to him. He was the best friend I had.

I guess it hit your mother and dad pretty hard. I will write them a letter tonight. I should have wrote them a long time ago but I haven't had much time. He never did write to me, I don't know why. Maybe he didn't get my letters. I wrote him three times, maybe he didn't get them.

I guess I am lucky by getting sent up here even tho it is awfully cold and lonesome, it is a lot better than going over there. I am glad you wrote to me, even tho my mother told me, all she knew, all she knew is what was in the papers. I don't know anything to write except I would have gave anything in the world if it hadn't happened. There isn't anything up here to write about except it is a place that there isn't anything to do. It is pretty cold now, not much snow yet. I guess I had better close and write your mother. I think I will take a furlough in January. Maybe I will see you & your husband.

So long for now,
Linard White

Appendix B: Tony K. Burris in The National Archive

The National Archive contains this summary of the life and military career of Tony K. Burris.

BURRIS, TONY K.

Rank and organization: Sergeant First Class, U.S. Army, Company L, 38th Infantry Regiment, 2d Infantry Division. Place and date: vicinity of Mundung-ni, Korea, 8 and 9 October 1951. Entered service at: Blanchard, Okla. Birth: Blanchard, Okla. G.O. No.: 84, 5 September 1952. Citation: Sfc. Burris, a member of Company L, distinguished himself by conspicuous gallantry and outstanding courage above and beyond the call of duty. On 8 October, when his company encountered intense fire from an entrenched hostile force, Sfc. Burris charged forward alone, throwing grenades into the position and destroying approximately 15 of the enemy. On the following day, spearheading a renewed assault on enemy positions on the next ridge, he was wounded by machinegun fire but continued the assault, reaching the crest of the ridge ahead of his unit and sustaining a second wound. Calling for a 57mm recoilless rifle team, he deliberately exposed himself to draw hostile fire and reveal the enemy position. The enemy machinegun emplacement was destroyed. The company then moved forward and prepared to assault other positions on the ridgeline. Sfc. Burris, refusing evacuation and submitting only to emergency [illegible] ... pressed attack led the assault against two more positions halted ... and destroyed the first ...

BURRIS, TONY K.

Rank and organization: Sergeant First Class, U.S. Army, Company L, 38th Infantry Regiment, 2d Infantry Division. Place and date: vicinity of Mundung-ni, Korea, 8 and 9 October 1951. Entered service at: Blanchard, Okla. Birth: Blanchard, Okla. G.O. No.: 84, 5 September 1952. Citation: Sfc. Burris, a member of Company L, distinguished himself by conspicuous gallantry and outstanding courage above and beyond the call of duty. On

October 8, when his company encountered intense fire from an entrenched hostile force, Sfc. Burris charged forward alone, throwing grenades into the position and destroying approximately 15 of the enemy. On the following day, spearheading a renewed assault on enemy positions on the next ridge, he was wounded by machinegun fire but continued the assault, reacing the crest of the ridge ahead of his unit and sustaining a second wound. Calling for a 57mm recoilless rifle team, he deliberately exposed himself to draw hostile fire and reveal the enemy position. The enemy machinegun emplacement was destroyed. The company then moved forward and prepared to assault the other positions on the ridgeline. Sfc. Burris, refusing evacuation and submitting only to emergency treatment, joined the unit in its renewed attack but fire from hostile emplacements halted the advance. Sfc. Burris rose to his feet, charged forward and destroyed the first emplacement with its heavy machinegun and crew of six men. Moving out to the next emplacement and throwing his last grenade, which destroyed the position, he fell mortally wounded by enemy fire. Inspired by his own consummate gallantry, his comrades renewed a spirited assault, which overran enemy positions and secured Hill 605, a strategic position in the battle for "Heartbreak Ridge." Sfc. Burris' indomitable fighting spirit, outstanding heroism, and gallant self-sacrifice reflect the highest glory upon himself, the infantry, and the U.S. Army.

TONY K. BURRIS

Sergeant First Class Tony Kenneth Burris is listed as the 59th soldier and the 92nd overall Korean War Medal of Honor recipient. Born on 30 May 1929 in Blanchard, Oklahoma, he was the third of ten children born to Samuel Sidney Burris, Jr. and the former Mable Agnes Curry. Burris grew up in Blanchard with his brothers and sisters (Loretta, Wanda Lou, Burnett, Joyce Joan, Karen Jane, twins Terry Doyce and Perry Royce, and twins Diana Judy and Catherine Jennifer). He attended the local public schools in Blanchard and graduated from Blanchard High School on 22 May 1947. With the outbreak of hostilities in Korea, Burris enlisted in the United States Army and completed basic combat training at Fort Riley, Kansas, and advanced individual training at Fort Belvoir, Virginia. Afterwards,

TONY K. BURRIS

Sergeant First Class Tony Kenneth Burris is listed as the 59th soldier and the 92nd overall Korean War Medal of Honor recipient. Born 30 May 1929 in Blanchard, Oklahoma, he was the third of ten children born to Samuel Sidney Burris, Jr. and the former Mable Agnes Curry. Burris grew up in Blanchard with his brothers and sisters (Loretta, Wanda Lou, Burnett, Joyce Joan, Karen Jane, twins Terry Doyce and Perry Royce, and twins Diana Judy and Catherine Jennifer). He attended the local public schools in Blanchard and graduated from Blanchard High School on 22 May 1947. With the outbreak of hostilities in Korea, Burris enlisted in the United States Army and completed basic combat training at Fort Riley, Kansas, and advanced individual training at Fort Belvoir, Virginia. Afterwards, he was deployed to the Korean Theater of Operations where he served as a rifleman with Company L of the 38th Infantry Regiment, 2nd Infantry Division. Burris quickly earned an enviable reputation as a combat leader and with only one year of service, he was advanced to the grade of sergeant first class. He was wounded in action on 12 February 1951, but was returned to duty on 29 March. Prior to the action that merited him the Medal of Honor, Burris had already been decorated with the Silver Star and two Purple Hearts. On 9 October 1951, he was wounded twice more before he was killed in the same action that would earn him the Medal of Honor. At an awards ceremony held at the Pentagon on 14 August 1952, Mr. Samuel S. Burris, Jr. formally accepted his son's posthumous Medal of Honor from General of the Army Omar N. Bradley (Chairman of the Joint Chiefs of Staff). During this same ceremony, posthumous Medal of Honor awards were also presented to the families of Sergeant LeRoy A. Mendonca and Private First Class David M. Smith. Burris is one of eighteen soldiers assigned to the 2nd Infantry Division that earned the Medal of Honor for heroism during the Korean War and one of two Korean War Medal of Honor recipients accredited to the state of Oklahoma. His other awards and decorations for service in Korea include the Good Conduct Medal, the National Defense Service Medal, the Korean Service Medal, the United Nations Service Medal, the Republic of Korea's Presidential Unit Citation, and the Combat Infantryman Badge. In separate ceremonies held at Fort Lewis, Washington, in August 1955 and June 1957 respectively, the Tony K. Burris Memorial Dayroom of Company L of the 38th Infantry Regiment was named in his honor and Burris Field was officially dedicated to his memory. As further tributes to his selfless acts of heroism, the Tony K. Burris US Army Reserve Center (located at Chickasha, Oklahoma) was officially memorialized in his honor on 25 September 1960 and Burris Hall (Building #2552, located on Main Post, US Army Garrison Yongsan, Seoul, South Korea) was named after him on 9 April 1962. Additionally, Observation Post Burris (located along the demilitarized zone) was named in his honor on 1 March 1971. This observation post was previously known as Mazie and was renamed in a ceremony hosted by Lieutenant General Edward L. Rowny, Commanding General of 1 Corps. It has since been released to the ROK Army. The Tony K. Burris VFW Post (located in his hometown of Blanchard, Oklahoma) also bears his name and in 1967, the Tony K. Burris Chapter #138 of the Noncommissioned Officers Association, with headquarters at Tinker Air Force Base, Oklahoma, was named for him. Also, Battery B of the 2nd Battalion/2nd Field Artillery (headquartered at Fort Sill, Oklahoma – "Home of the US Army Field Artillery") has served as the Fort Sill Salute Battery since 1971. Each of its seven M101 salute howitzers bears the name of a Medal of Honor recipient from the state of Oklahoma. Included among these honors is Tony K. Burris. His remains were eventually returned to the United States and buried with full military honors at the Blanchard Cemetery (which is located in his hometown).

Appendix C: Hill 605

Tony's Battalion led the attack on Hill 605[3] as detailed in this excerpt from a Command Report. Tony played a major role in this battle as detailed in his Medal of Honor citation.

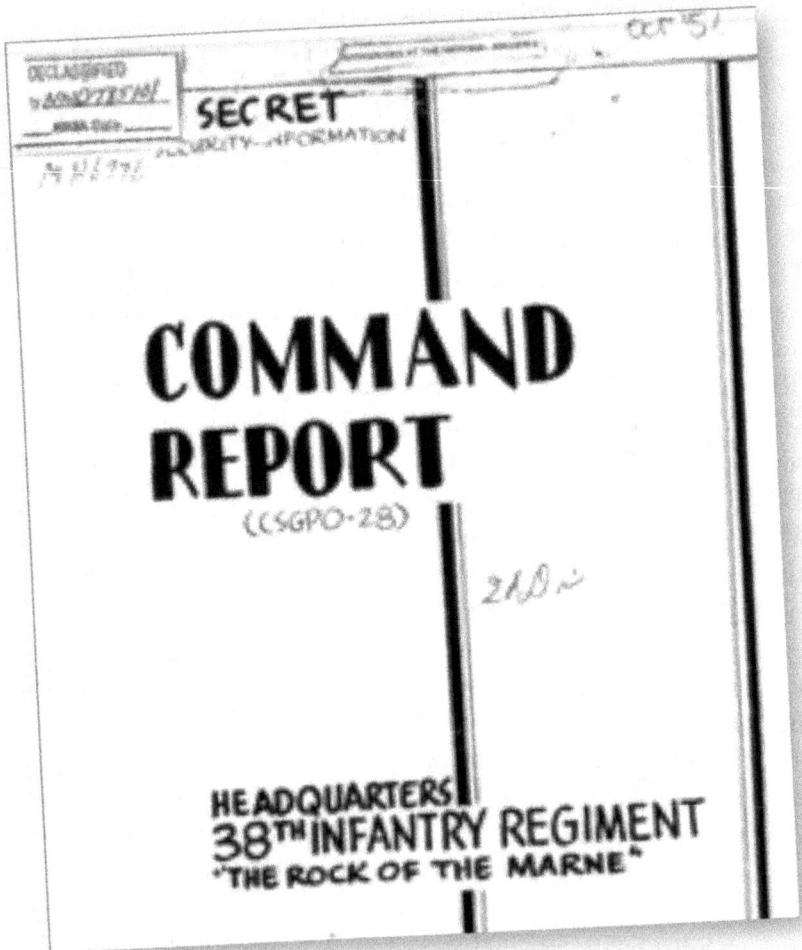

SECRET
SECURITY INFORMATION

COMMAND REPORT
(CSGPO-28)

HEADQUARTERS
38TH INFANTRY REGIMENT
"THE ROCK OF THE MARNE"

---

3 Hill 605 is now in the demilitarized zone between North and South Korea.

Excerpt from *Command Report*, page 4

*During the period 8 to 11 October, the First Battalion
occupied positions in the vicinity of (DT093305) as
Regimental Reserves. The Third Battalion moved out for
Objective "1" at 0600 hours, on the 8th receiving only light
resistance they reported they were on objective "1" by 1120
hours on that date.*

*Due to faulty terrain features on the map this was later
discovered to be an erroneous report and at 0910 hours, on
9 October the Third Battalion was again moving forward
towards Objective "1". Their position at this time was in the
vicinity of (DT101384) and (DT111390) with Company
I in the vicinity of (DT115764). They continued their
advance moving forward under enemy mortar, artillery and
machine gun fire. At 1235 hours they received a counter
attack from the ridge line of Hill 905, and the ridge line of
Hill 605. Lead elements placed artillery fire with excellent
results and the battalion continued their advance. Again on
the 10th the Third Battalion attacked toward their objective,
mopping up fingers on Hill 605 and extended from Hill 605
to vicinity of (DT114407). The Netherland Detachment
was in contact with that battalion until it was relieved on
the 12th, at 1800 hours, by the 9th Regiment.*

Discussion Questions

1. What might Tony have become had he not gone to war?

2. What would Tony's life have been like had he survived the war?

3. What is courage? What does it take to be a hero? Why did Tony repeatedly go alone against entrenched positions?

4. Once committed to front line action, soldiers needed to be captured, wounded, frostbitten, or killed in order go home. They were too valuable and thus became expendable. Is this a reasonable policy?

Donor Acknowledgements

We appreciate the support of the following donors:

Phil Holloway

Sherry N. Ramsey

Glen, Mary &
  Dylan Wilson

John Stewart

Caroline Barbara Stewart

Teresa A. & Carlee Wilson

Ralph & Patricia F. Edwards

Twila & Larry Wilson

Jerrie K. Smith

Lizbeth Stringer

Robert G. Purvis

Thanks, also, to others who provided us images of Tony's life and family, and to the National Archives of the United States, for the use of materials to help us tell the wartime story of Tony K. Burris.

www.ingramcontent.com/pod-product-compliance
Lightning Source LLC
Chambersburg PA
CBHW070819100426
42813CB00033B/3436/J